Body Intelligence Meditation

Body Intelligence Meditation

Finding presence
through embodiment

Ged Sumner

SINGING
DRAGON

LONDON AND PHILADELPHIA

Figures 4.1, 5.2, 5.5, 7.1, 7.2, 9.1, 9.2, 10.1, 10.3, 10.4, 10.5, 10.6, 14.3, 14.6, 14.7, 15.3 are taken from *Anatomy of the human body* by Henry Gray (20th ed., thoroughly rev. and re-edited by Warren H. Lewis), Philadelphia, Lea & Febiger, 1918. Reproduced by kind permission of www. bartleby.com.

First published in 2014
by Singing Dragon
an imprint of Jessica Kingsley Publishers
73 Collier Street
London N1 9BE, UK
and
400 Market Street, Suite 400
Philadelphia, PA 19106, USA

www.singingdragon.com

Library of Congress Cataloging in Publication Data
Sumner, Ged, author.
  Body intelligence meditation : finding presence through embodiment / Ged Sumner.
    pages cm
  Includes bibliographical references and index.
  ISBN 978-1-84819-174-7 (alk. paper)
  1. Meditation--Therapeutic use. 2. Meditation--Physiologica aspects. 3. Mind and body. I. Title.
  RC489.M43S86 2014
  615.8'528--dc23
                                    2014004229

British Library Cataloguing in Publication Data
A CIP catalogue record for this book is available from the British Library

ISBN 978 1 84819 174 7
eISBN 978 0 85701 121 3

Printed and bound in Great Britain

Contents

Preface

This book has emerged out of my practice and teaching of Biodynamic Craniosacral Therapy (BCST), Elemental Chi Kung and Living Anatomy. These disciplines provide remarkable insights into how the human body functions. Most of those insights are from BCST and its unique holistic view of the body. The development within BCST has been spectacular; however, it is a small bodywork community that is not well known. With BCST, a cutting edge around touch and perception has brought about a highly embodied way of healing that generates astounding results. It's not easy to explain, though, as the practitioner facilitates the client's body to self-adjust and there is more a state of presence than a state of action. Most people who experience this have very profound reactions.

I've practised many different forms of meditation and notice in retrospect how my initial explorations led to a dissociation from my body. It took me a while to realize that becoming present to the body was the way towards deeper and more dynamic meditation. Movement towards our structure, tissues, cells and fluids brings us into the cauldron of life.

Books on meditation and related philosophies comprise highly diverse ideas that are often contradictory and can be highly confusing. Many meditational methods seek to transcend the body, and in so doing they encourage a shift away from it. Many other methods prescribe an awareness of the body but don't give enough insights or explanations of how to achieve such awareness. For me, meditation is a journey into felt sense awareness and the natural forces of health within the body. So becoming present through sensitive relationship to the body opens up a tremendous amount of energy, and a new consciousness starts to reveal itself. The body is our anatomy and physiology, and the mind is not separate from it but rather based upon and within it.

This book attempts to bring you into a refined relationship with your body through understanding and appreciating your anatomy as a living, intelligent expression. You are your physiology, and your physiology is totally remarkable and has depths and functions that modern science is only just starting to appreciate. This is invaluable in charting the sea of awareness and sensations within us. As we grow in awareness of our bodies, we sink more deeply into its mysteries.

HOW TO USE THIS BOOK

The recommendation is to work your way through the whole book from start to finish. That way you will be able to assess your system's change of health in detail. Then go back and concentrate on the chapters you found difficult (without forgetting the chapters you found more accessible).

People vary considerably in their natural rhythms. Try meditating at different times of the day to see how your body responds. Many people feel good meditating in the early morning or early evening. It's important that you find the time that suits you best. Furthermore, the space you meditate in can have a considerable effect on you. Ideally, it needs to be a quiet place with no distractions and where you feel secure.

You don't need to sit with crossed legs. Try experimenting with different positions (e.g. kneeling, sitting on chairs or stools, sitting on bolsters with different leg arrangements or even standing, which can be particularly powerful). In all cases the important thing is for the body to be well aligned and comfortable. It will not be helpful if you create strain such that 10 minutes into the meditation the body is in pain. Determine a position of ease so that your body can become still and relax.

Most of the meditations in this book are designed to be 10–15 minutes long. Each meditation has a particular intention, and therefore you will be active in your awareness, opening up to various aspects of your body. Once you have made a connection to the subject of the meditation, it's natural to drift into a neutral state of mind such that you are not focused on the structures of your body in the same way that you were when you began the meditation. Often you will transition into a more expanded state of awareness, which is OK. You may find yourself continuing with the meditation for much longer than 10–15 minutes, and that the experience has become organic and spontaneous. In meditation, the body starts to reveal various facets of its complex nature.

You will notice that there are many anatomical terms used in this book. If you are not familiar with any of them, simply use an Internet search engine (e.g. Google) to obtain images and explanations so that you can become more familiar with particular parts of the body. There's so much information on hand to help you understand your own body.

The body doesn't respond well to strong focus or intention. The meditations are worded as an invitation to the body to reveal itself. So maintaining an awareness that isn't pushy is really important. Listening to the body will bring about greater perspective and insight. Sometimes you might find that you are struggling to feel the subject of the meditation. Try to be patient with your body and understand that it might take several attempts before you perceive the anatomy.

Many of the meditations are structural in their intention, but don't be surprised if the body drops into a fluid state while you are meditating. This is therapeutic across the whole anatomical system, so don't resist it. You might feel like you are losing your relationship to the finer aspects of your anatomy, because that relationship is being replaced with a more systemic relationship, and in the fluid state profound reorganizations occur.

Your body will almost certainly readjust itself during the meditations. This is to be expected and sometimes it can be quite dramatic. Literally joints can reposition themselves, organs can shift their physiology and the body can vibrate or shake. Try to allow these movements to take place in an organic way. They will come and go. Changes in breath and circulation are commonplace as well as the speeding up and slowing down of the nervous system. Surges of energy, changes in your body size and shape, and shifts in your thought processes can take place. Sometimes the effects aren't so pleasant; nausea, headaches and other pains can reveal themselves. Understand that these are expressions of your body processing patterns held latently in your physiology, and they will pass. All these expressions are indications that your health is being activated in a new way. You will quickly begin to notice that your body feels more whole and vital. Your mind will become calmer and you will be more creative.

If you wish to pursue this approach to meditation in more depth, information on a weekend program is offered at www.BImeditation. com. The program presents all the information in this book in more detail and in a group setting. The four weekends consist of step-by-step processes to initiate a deep change in your system.

Note that all meditations in this book are available as audio files that can be downloaded for free from www.BImeditation.com.

CHAPTER 1

What Is Real?

The cerebral cortex is a marvellous structure that is responsible for the wonder of thinking, perception and reflection. We live in a world that praises and rewards intellectual intelligence. Thinking is a big business and developments in modern technology have increased the strain on the brain. We communicate and process information more often and more efficiently than in the past. Words and ideas fill us. We now learn in a short time things our forefathers would have taken millennia to discover. We have created a modern civilization that has taken us beyond existing just to meet our basic needs. People in industrialized countries live a lot longer and possess much more than ever before. Much of this has derived from the amazing development of the human brain.

But has the brain gotten 'too big'? Has the mind become too dominant? Is our thinking and intellectualizing out of control? The world of thought seems to utterly dominate the human species.

With the growth of the human brain and the shift to a cerebral existence, some things have gotten lost. You can see it everywhere in society. People are locked into a thought-based reality. No one seems to be present as they stare blank faced, lost in a world of thought. It's as if Western culture has become addicted to thinking and to the power of intellect. At the same time, our idea of successful survival has shifted from the idea of meeting our basic needs to an obsession with consumerism. Survival is now about success: being famous, making money and owning bigger and better houses and cars.

WHAT IMPACT DOES ALL OF THIS HAVE?

While the mind is creating a constant stream of thoughts, our bodies respond by creating chemical and structural reactions just as incessantly. The overall effect on physical and mental health is disastrous. For example, the focus on external success and material wealth has created an increase in anxiety and neurosis. It's quite clear that the human organism in modern society is under unbearable strain. Many people are becoming ill and dysfunctional. As a craniosacral therapist, I've spent the past 20 years putting my hands on people in clinics, and 90% of people fall into this category to some degree or other. They are just coping, and their bodies are hyperactive (i.e. hearts and brains racing, everything accelerated to just get through the barrage of the modern world). It's obvious that something is out of balance. The pressure on the average person is very high and is not sustainable. People are malfunctioning.

Within a short time human development has accelerated at an exponential rate. Just two generations takes us back to the 1940s and 1950s, a period when the world was very different. My father had an average job from the 1950s through the 1970s and supported a family of five on one wage. He worked nine to five, 5 days a week. That sounds almost utopian today. Unless you are earning a lot of money, that way of life is no longer possible for the average person. So in order to sustain a basic lifestyle, both partners need to work or people need to have multiple jobs. Many people work extra-long hours and 6 or 7 days a week.

The insanity of the pace of modern life means that everyone is in survival mode and the body's resources are empty. The challenge to both society and the human physiology is enormous. In a world dominated by sensory barrage, environmental stress and life lived at breakneck speed, statistics show that stress-related and 'lifestyle' diseases are on the rise. More people than ever are now suffering from:

- irritable bowel syndrome

- diabetes (late onset)

- asthma

- depression

- hyperthyroidism

- skin conditions

- obesity

- high blood pressure.

Living in thoughts takes you away from awareness of your body. Being aware of your body keeps you in the present. Having a deep and sensitive connection with your body brings you into closer contact with your feelings and leads to a clarity of mind that will allow you to disengage from the *conditioned* mind.

ACHIEVING HOMEOSTASIS

How can we reclaim our body's wisdom and stop listening to our neurotic minds? Is there a place where the mind can rest and thoughts do not consume us? Can the body become calmer and not so driven by the mind? The answer is yes, and the solution can be found right in our own biology. The answer is homeostasis.

Homeostasis is the ability of an organism or cell to maintain internal equilibrium by adjusting its physiological processes. When we achieve homeostasis, the whole system functions in a balanced way. That is the optimal state to attain, and the beginning of that journey is to become deeply acquainted with your body through the felt sense. This in turn will uncover a special power of the mind: its natural ability to be still.

The felt sense is what we use to feel internal body sensations. There's a whole sensory system dedicated to your felt sense. You can become supersensitive to the body by attuning to it and in doing so drop into the most remarkable states of awareness. The mind goes quiet. The brain and central nervous system deeply settle and you start to perceive with a clarity that is free of thoughts.

What might be amazing to many people is the fact that the mind doesn't need to think. Its natural state is to be still and present, and a still mind is a listening mind that can open to the body's sensations without distraction. You discover that you still exist without thoughts. In fact, you become *more* existent and start to find a state of bliss that all of nature shares. There's a natural bliss from being in deep connection to your body and a state of homeostasis. So harnessing this ability is vital.

Homeostasis will bring optimal health both mentally and physically. The benefits are enormous. Your behaviour will change, and you will relate to others and to your environment differently. You will become balanced in your perception of things. You will feel happy. You will be better able to listen to your body's intelligence. There's a wisdom within you that has taken you from a single cell to the most complex organism in the world. That's how smart your body is – much smarter than any series of thoughts or ideas. Your body is life, and its physiology includes an amazing brain that can be a balanced thinking machine.

When you are in touch with your body, you can feel all the nuances of your being. That's the key – to be in touch with yourself and not in a mental fog. You will start to notice many things as you relate to your body through being receptive. You will notice how your posture is. You don't need to be measured. You just feel it because you are able to listen to your joint receptors. You can feel when certain foods aren't right for you. You can tell if you are not breathing well, because you don't remain disconnected from it. You can tell if you are upset or repressing emotions, because you are in contact with them. Your body no longer needs to 'scream' these things at you.

Developing the felt sense takes practice. This book is a practical guide on how to develop the felt sense through meditation, and it also looks at what lies behind the constant hubbub of the body and mind. It reveals a landscape that is in the background of our awareness and reconnects us to our biology. The body is not an automaton, it's a highly sensitive living creature that is *you*. Through body intelligence meditation, your body can be experienced so completely that you become a vibrant sentient being rather than just a thinking apparatus. Once this occurs, you will be in harmony with the same life force that guides the entire universe. You will be able to feel its power as well as your innate sea of bliss, which will lead you into ecstatic union with your own life.

CHAPTER 2

Felt Sense Awareness

We live in a sea of sensation. Our ability to sense the world within us and around us is extraordinary. We have a huge array of sensory receptors throughout our body that can exquisitely reveal subtle internal movement and states as well as continuously inform us about our environment. Most of this information comes from our general senses. These are the biggest collection of receptors and nerve fibres in the body and represent 90% of our incoming information flow. Much of it is what we call *felt sense*.

Generally, we are powerfully oriented to experiencing the world through the traditional five senses of hearing, taste, smell, touch and, in particular, sight. Our felt sense, however, is something that is much less recognized. Felt sense entails an entirely different kind of awareness that doesn't involve cognitive processes. It's intuitive and more about feeling how you are, sensing others and feeling your environment. We all have an awareness of this to a degree, but few people can fathom its depth.

How aware are you of your body? How do you feel it? It's surprising that we can be in our bodies without being fully related to them. In fact, most people are more interested in objects outside the body than they are in their own body. The very thing everyone lives in is so poorly understood at both a knowledge and an experiential level. Biology is just another subject taught in school. If you take away beliefs, all we are is our biology, and the biggest part of that is our felt sense receptivity.

YOU ARE 'RECEPTIVE'

The word 'sensorium' is a great word. It means the sum of an organism's perceptions, the 'seat of sensation'. Sensations and perceptions are entwined. How you sense is how you perceive. We all look similar; we have arms and legs and move in similar ways. But one of the big differences is how deeply we are in relationship to our felt sense, which is the most defining part of us. Most of our felt sense comes from receptors that monitor movements throughout the body and, apart from muscle receptors (which are a small part of our sensory system), they are all located in the connective tissues of the body – that is, the ligaments, tendons, fascia and membranes.

Here's a list of the different kinds of receptors in the body:

- Ampullae of Lorenzin respond to electric fields, salinity and temperature, but function primarily as electroreceptors.

- Baroreceptors respond to pressure in blood vessels.

- Chemoreceptors respond to chemical stimuli.

- Electromagnetic receptors respond to electromagnetic waves.

- Hydroreceptors respond to changes in humidity.

- Mechanoreceptors respond to mechanical stress or strain.

- Nociceptors respond to damage to body tissues leading to pain perception.

- Osmoreceptors respond to the osmolarity of fluids (such as in the hypothalamus).

- Photoreceptors respond to light.

- Proprioceptors provide the sense of position.

- Thermoreceptors respond to temperature (either heat, cold or both).

Not only are we responsive to information about our internal world, we also have receptors for light, humidity, temperature and electromagnetic waves which are all about monitoring our external environment. Then there are the so-called 'special senses', which also involve the world around us. So your body and mind are tracking both the external world and your internal world. It makes sense, therefore, that the more present in your body you are, the more receptive you are to your internal state. The receptors produce the 'feeling' of your body and the 'feeling' of the external environment. The information flow from these receptors can be disrupted so that we become less aware of felt sense perceptions. This can come from physical injury, congestion or dissociation.

WHAT ARE YOU MOST AWARE OF IN YOUR BODY?

The top three places we are mostly associated with in our bodies in terms of felt sense are: (1) face, (2) hands and (3) feet. This is due mainly to how the brain organizes its sensory priorities. It needs to be in constant communication with all of these places because they are so important to the daily functioning of the body. For example, the face is where all of our cranial sense organs reside. (Let's include the ears with the face.) It's essential to the processes of eating, breathing and talking – so there's a lot going on there! The hands are particularly important as we are highly manual. Most of the functionality in our daily lives requires complex hand-and-finger coordination. We walk using the feet, and the brain closely monitors them for balance and support. They are, after all, the foundation of the body.

There are big areas of the sensory cortex dedicated to these three places. The rest of the body takes up a lot less brain area (Figure 2.1) and can often slip off into the background. A lot of our days are spent with just the hands and the face, and if we are not careful, this behaviour becomes ingrained. In other words, we drop out of felt sense of the rest of the body and become 'just faces and hands'. This is happening more and more as we become so deeply immersed in a digital world which prioritizes eyes, ears and hands. We speak to each other face to face less than ever. We watch screens and tap furiously with the fingers. Plus we are thinking constantly. So you could say life is mostly about hands, eyes and pre-frontal cortex. It's no wonder the world is becoming more and more heady and less and less body. How else could it be? We are missing whole segments of the spectrum of life and becoming increasingly myopic.

LETTING GO OF TENSION OR RELEASING YOUR HANDS, HEAD AND FACE

If your brain is very interested in your head, hands and face, then if you brought those areas into a state of relaxation, your brain would relax, too. Relaxation is what we need to do to feel ourselves. The body struggles to feel itself when it is tense. Relaxing is therefore not a small thing – it's essential for life. Often relaxation is talked about as if it's trivial, but it's actually a movement towards homeostasis. The meditation described below will bring this about.

Meditation: homunculus

Sit for a couple of minutes and come into whole-body awareness. Do this by opening up to the whole volume of your body. Be interested in your hands. Sensation in your hands should come to you instantly. Put the back of your hands on your thighs and let each finger relax in turn. Start with your thumbs. Now relax the palms of your hands. There are lots of small muscles in the webbing of the hand that can be held tight. Do the same with the base of the hand and the wrist. Let go, too, of any tension in your forearms. All of these places can be held in deep tension often without knowing it. As your hands relax, notice the effect on your nervous system and whole body.

Be interested in your feet. Go through the same process with your feet. This time let go of tension in the centre within the arch. This allows tensions to dissolve in the webbing of the feet. Let go around the heel, too, as that dissolves tensions in the tarsal bones, which can get compressed. Now relax the soles of the feet all the way up to the Achilles tendon and the ankle. Lastly, let the toes relax. Again, notice the effect on your whole system.

Be interested in your mouth. Let go of tension in your lower jaw and throat. Just let the jaw hang. Do the same inside the mouth, so that the tongue and the floor and roof of the mouth relax. Finally, let your lips soften. Notice how that relieves tension in your whole face and once again in the whole body.

This meditation is a great way to wind your brain down quickly.

Figure 2.1 Homunculus

COMING INTO OUR WHOLE BODY

If we can open up to the rest of our senses and come out of our face and hands, we can reclaim the rest of our body. The first step is to find the rest of our musculoskeletal system; this is our voluntary system. We should become more conscious of this system as we more consciously engage with it. Then we can start to find our deeper parts, our anatomical cavities and organ systems, which are running in the background.

What are the biggest movements in our body? Breathing is number one: the whole ribcage moves, the lungs inflate and the diaphragm rises and falls along with lots of muscular movements to make it smooth and efficient. Most of the body in one way or another is involved in, or affected by, breathing. Even so, it's not uncommon for people to be blissfully unaware of it in their daily life. Not only that, but they are actually not able to feel how their breathing is, so that they can give you detailed feedback on it without going to a health professional to find out how well they are breathing. Diagnose yourself by simply listening to your breath. By itself, it's the most powerful way to connect with felt sense awareness. If your breathing is poor and conflicted, your felt sense awareness will diminish because the movement of your breath has an effect on the entire body (see Chapter 7).

Number two is the movement of the heart and blood. The heart makes strong movements in the chest and to some degree the body filters these movements out from our everyday consciousness. But we are meant to have the ability to connect with its movement at will. You shouldn't need to be told how your heart is, you should be able to *feel* how it is. The sensory apparatus is there to inform you. How can you miss the movement of 9–12 pints of liquid around your system? A drop of blood moves around your body in less than 2 minutes! Your whole body is awash with it. So tuning into blood has got to be an astonishing felt sense shift (see Chapter 12).

Number three is the movement of the gut. We eat and our digestion is a considerable process that principally involves the stomach, the small intestine and colon. In addition, the liver, gallbladder and pancreas become highly active. It should feel like a turbine turning on. The biggest gross movement is the peristalsis of your small intestine. This is metres of tube squirming and rippling in your abdomen. Felt sense awareness of this means you know how well your digestion is performing. You don't need a test for it. If you listen to your gut with an open presence it will tell you what to feed it.

ARE YOU DISSOCIATED?

Presence and dissociation are at opposite ends of the spectrum. When you are present, you are highly attuned to your body and therefore your felt sense awareness is high. When you are dissociated, you are less present and are numb to your body (Figure 2.2).

Below is a meditation on the skin. Your skin is an extraordinary felt sense organ, and its health and communication with your nervous system is defining for your felt sense. Follow the meditation guidelines so that you can listen in to the health of your skin. Your skin is your most sensitive organ. Learning to relate to it more deeply means you become more sensitive. Mapping the skin with your felt sense awareness is very revealing. The skin is a tapestry of feelings and sensations.

Meditation: skin presence

Find your skin. Your face is one of the most sensitive parts of your body and one of which you are very aware. So open up to the outer layer of your face. This outer layer has a different feel from what lies beneath it. You can feel a denser part of your face, which is bones, joints and muscles, but notice that covering them is the skin, which has quite a different feel to it. It's lighter and electrical. Plus it's sheet-like in structure, so track it across your face with your awareness, back to your ears and up to your forehead. Do the same with the skin under your hair; it sweeps back across the head to the ridge at the back of your head and top of your neck. Notice the different felt sense of the skin in the face compared with the skin at the back of the head. The skin is designed with a layer of fatty superficial fascia underneath it to give it an insulation and a unique mobility. The skin is very pliable because of this layer, which also makes the skin feel like it's floating. If you think of your skin as one big floating antenna, that will give you a sense of its quality and function. Even though we are so used to seeing and hearing the world around us, we can also *feel* it with our skin. Try feeling the environment with your skin.

Continue opening up to your skin on the rest of your body. Do it slowly so that you can concentrate on connecting with the skin on your limbs and the skin on the front and back of the torso. Once you've done that, purposefully open up to the whole skin. As you sit with the sensations, you will start to notice that certain parts of the skin are very 'feelable' and certain parts are less so, and most importantly some areas may be absent or feel numb. For some reason you are dissociated from these areas. It could be that there has been damage to that part of the skin, or through difficult experiences that part of the body has closed down its sensory flow or the brain is simply not recording it. In any event, there has been a reduction in your felt sense awareness and your body is less informed and you are less present.

If you repeatedly practise this meditation on the skin, you can reclaim your full felt sense, and as you do, notice how your relationship to your body changes.

BIOLOGY OF TRAUMA

The body at one level is really elementary. We respond like the simplest organisms on the planet – fungal spores, bacteria, protoplasm or slime mould. If there's danger, we all contract. It's totally instinctive in us down to our cells and down to our cytoplasm. So there's no choice. It's what all living things do. Humans are no different, even if we think we are. We are ruled by our biology. The problem occurs when we try to come out of contraction; it's often not so simple. We are complex, have big brains, have buried limbic systems beneath miles of cerebral hemispheres and our socialization has trained us out of letting go of the biological charges around alarm states. It's not acceptable to start weeping profusely or jerking your body around and convulsing as a way to recover from a difficult event – so in it stays and we remain contractile. Then our postures change and our body systems have to adjust, and suddenly we think and perceive differently. What remains often is anxiety overlaid with patterns of deep tension. In time, the original trauma details are forgotten and the charge turns into a general anxiety towards anything, that is, it gets displaced onto people and situations that are not part of the original experience. What you have now is a malfunctioning human being.

All of these states are well described in post-traumatic stress disorder. In short, if the traumatic experience is not resolved, it becomes lodged in your system, your behaviour and biology are changed and you become neurotic and sometimes psychotic. The body becomes ill and often develops symptoms of disorder that can emerge as many well-known conditions. So what we are looking at here is often the cause of illness. It's a huge phenomenon that has largely been unrecognized and misunderstood.

How can we become healthier?

The first thing is to understand what's going on with you. Illness has been symptomized within an inch of its life and that has led to a culture of superficiality. What's behind the symptoms? Why are they being generated? These are the questions to ask. The body just doesn't malfunction for no reason. Health approaches that only treat symptoms are not helpful around this. A broader look at the body and mind as a whole is needed. We are not little bits of body but one holistic system that functions as a unit. Psychosomatic explanations are very helpful. What happens when we experience profound loss and we are not able to grieve in the way our bodies need? What happens to the repressed emotions? The body can retain emotional patterns in its physiology. Emotions are cells and molecules, not something separate from the physical body. They are linked to the nervous and endocrine systems and lead to neuroendocrine imbalances if there is emotional constraint. Humans are emotional creatures and repression doesn't do the body any good.

The other thing to do is recognize the symptoms of nervous system imbalance. This is at the centre of most imbalances in the body. What is the tone of your nervous system? For example, is it running fast? When we react, we react from our cells but also from our neuroendocrine system. We have a special response in us that includes a whole nervous network called the autonomic nervous system, and we have special endocrine hormones that get secreted. Both of these factors produce our response to danger. It's generally a highly adrenalized state that includes a high-energy nervous charge and lots of heat and high metabolism. It's how the body gears up.

We've all had this experience. The body is designed for this system to fire up and then discharge, but if it doesn't discharge, it stays in the body as a background state. The body is basically still in flight or fight, but we have now normalized around it. This state is called hyperarousal and it's currently one of the most common states in the modern world. Many symptoms spin off from this as time goes by: paranoia, anxiety, hypervigilance, insomnia, digestive malfunction, shallow breathing, musculoskeletal tensions and high blood pressure. All are very common and familiar symptoms for billions of people on the planet. Basically, relaxing and remaining calm are almost impossible states to achieve while these symptoms persist.

Finally, if we start to relate to the expressions of health in the body, we can begin to make changes at the most fundamental level.

BIOLOGY OF HEALTH

The most significant expression in the body is generated by our health, which dwarfs everything else. Even if you are tired and in pain, or have a strong pathology, feelings surrounding your health are always present. The question shouldn't be 'What is health?' but rather 'What does health feel like?' We all know the feeling of being well. It creates a buoyant, light state that makes us feel happy. The body is fluid and easy. Every cell is highly dynamic and there is constant movement within us. This is the movement of health. The biology of health feels uplifting. Cell energy, the natural creative force within us, shines forth and we start to glow.

Meditation: wholeness and health

This is the most powerful meditation in this book. Open up to a sense of your whole body. It doesn't matter if you can't feel the whole of it. It's about coming into some sense of your whole system. The body is one system, one unit of function, and even though we understand it as consisting of lots of parts, in reality the parts don't exist. The body is a continuum of movements and structures that work together. Even when there is dysfunction, there is a huge movement towards whole-body communication and motion. This is where our health lies – not in one single part, such as the brain or the heart, but in the totality of movement and function. Try sitting with an awareness that is open to the movement of the whole. It takes practice. Your mind has been oriented to the particular parts since you were born. It's part of the nature of things to move out of wholeness and towards a relationship to individual things. After all, our lives are taken up with survival. Feeding and protecting the body and the complexity of human civilization has resulted in movement away from wholeness. Modern life seems to do that very powerfully. When you move towards simplicity and nature, you start to move towards your wholeness and the feeling of health increases. Going on holiday is a great example. Upon de-stressing, relaxing and being close to the sea or in nature, suddenly everyone feels much better and refreshed. You can maintain that feeling of health by constantly being aware of your body as a whole. It's a challenging practice in a challenging world, but for every effort towards it the body surges towards you with its fullness. You had this experience when you were a baby and a child. The baby and the child are in their totality of experience, and that's where health lies, in our 'baby' state. So the meditation involves constantly reminding yourself that you are whole. It's about constantly opening up to the entirety of the body and the continuum of sensations that are running within us.

Being whole means feeling the *sensation* of wholeness. Being whole generates your full health, and the feeling of health is something to observe and experience fully. Don't let it pass you by and don't forget it. Revel in the feeling of health, and the physiology of the body can take it up as a permanent state, not a transitory one. So when you sit in meditation, orient yourself to becoming aware of the whole body as a unit of function, that is, a continuous flowing-motion dynamic. You need to train your mind to let go of orientation to individual structures or layers in the body and open up to the movement of the whole. Then there is a surge of health and bliss. The body loves being seen for its wholeness. Through practice, you can reprogram your system to default to its natural state of health.

CHAPTER 3

Dynamic Stillness

A state of deep calm seems to be part of nature and our make-up. The great mystery of life is the juxtaposition of constant motion and stillness. How do these two states go together? It's actually not such a conundrum. The term *dynamic stillness* defines it. We are a blend of the two, dynamism and stillness. You can drop into a state of stillness and experience the fury of motion that's going on inside of you. The mind can be still and the body can be still, too, but the huge hive of activity in the physiology of the body is a constant. The more you can drop into that motion with stillness, the more you will start to experience states of bliss and presence.

Stillness for many is a mystery. The constant hum and activity of the physiology is comprehensible, but how do we understand stillness? Is it even physical? There's nothing in the body that is ever still. Everything in physical and energetic form exhibits motion until the day it dies. The universe is in constant flux. There is, however, a backdrop of stillness of which we are a part. It takes the form of quiescence of mind, deep rest of body, re-balancing of the body's biochemistry and structural alignment. Stillness is formless; it's a state of being, and being is in a marriage with form. The two conditions are entwined. One is the form of the universe and the other is the formless. The two coruscate together like yin and yang.

The way to the formless is through form. The deeper your relationship to your form, the more you discover your formlessness.

The more felt sense aware you become, the more connected to your stillness you become. So meditation isn't about leaving the body and escaping, it's about sinking more deeply into it. Embodiment is the path to connecting with the universe, and the body is the sensory machine for feeling your environment.

What happens when you sit or stand and your body is unmoving? There is an arising sense of health and well-being. The power of your body is released to express itself without being caught up in movement. Movement obfuscates us from the hidden force of health. When we stop and wait it starts to surface, and when it does, it wants to create balance. The body remembers unresolved negative experiences and these manifest latently as strains, tensions patterns, difficult emotions and pain. The arising health starts to act on this fallout from such experiences. So, often in the beginning meditation is turbulent, with lots of internal physical adjustments, which commonly create spontaneous movements that can be felt and expressed either subtly or grossly.

The physiology of the body loves the opportunity for higher orders of homeostasis, that is, the balanced integration of systems in the body. The greater the body's homeostasis, the better cell activity, neuroendocrine balance and therefore basic functions of breathing, digestion and circulation. So bringing your body into physical stillness produces a revolution in your physiology. The important thing is to surrender to your body's intelligence. Be disciplined about bringing the body into physical stillness and be patient as the body starts a natural process of renewal. Stay with an awareness of both the forces of health and the forces of condition (injury, trauma, illness, etc.) that exist within you, because both are part of who you are. As you continue, you will notice that your deeper health resides within you as a state of stillness. Getting in contact with this stillness generates all the physical changes described above.

So what does stillness actually feel like? Stillness is a dynamo. It's a state of deep residing that is simple and full of life. It underlies the mind and thoughts slow to a stop. Stillness infuses the body so that there is no longer a need to breathe. Your breathing slows down, often to a stop. The whole body lets go into it so that you feel suspended in a field of stillness. The body then goes into a state of peace and bliss as all its cells are bathed in this stillness.

As your practice becomes regular, you find that part of your awareness is always in relationship to stillness, as if it's in the background of everything – behind all movements of nature, behind your daily activities, behind your thoughts and emotions.

SITTING OR STANDING WITHOUT MOVEMENT

Let your body be still in a sitting position. Make sure you can stay in a posture that is sustainable for half an hour. Don't sit in a crossed-legs position if it's not easy for you, as creating strain will hinder your process. The important thing is to assume an aligned posture that allows you to relax, because then it's easy to be still. Kneeling and sitting with your legs under a low stool can be very conducive to your vertebral column being balanced. Sitting upright in a chair with your feet on the ground is also fine. The challenge is to let your physical body become still without constraint. Purposely let go of tension in your shoulder and hip joints, and relax your hands and feet. This is such a powerful way of letting the body become neutral and unencumbered in sitting. The periphery lets go, and that in turn influences the core of the body. Now let your jaw drop and tensions dissolve in your face, including relaxing your eyes. All of this has a deep effect on the nervous system. Your mind can't slow down with all these tensions in your body. Next, feel into your ribcage and ask it to relax. And finally, let go of your abdominal wall.

The body is now neutral in its sitting posture and you can easily be physically still. As the body remains in this state, the nervous system and mind start to relax and become still without effort.

Meditation: stillness

You need reminding about stillness. Modern life has little interest in it. We have all become imprinted with an urge to activity that is both an overbearing work ethic and a neurotic need to be scintillated. Being still is very unfashionable and uncool. Once you glimpse your innate stillness, your body will respond powerfully to it and each time you open up to it, there will be a much stronger connection.

Sit and let your body become calm, as described above. Recognize the tremendous activity in your body. How can we ever get tired with so much energy and movement taking place within us? Let's open up to the underlying stillness gradually. Start with your heart. The movement of the heart is constant. You couldn't name a structure that is more caught up in motion. As you feel the movement of the heart, simply open up to the movement taking place within a field of stillness. Even if that doesn't make any sense to your rational mind, open up to it. Do the same with the other big movement in your body, your breathing. Be with the felt sense of the ribcage and diaphragm moving, but again open up to the movement taking place in a field of stillness. The body will start automatically reorganizing when you do this. Notice the effect on your body. Lastly, notice the furious activity of your brain and thoughts, and open up to stillness as an intrinsic component of that. Again, you will feel something as you do it.

Stay with that for a while and then simply open up to your whole body being part of a field of stillness that embraces everything, so that all activity within you is part of the stillness. Now listen and feel as your system becomes modified by the stillness. Everything slows down. Breath, heart and mind all gear down and something sparks up in the body as a whole. It's a dynamic energy that comes through your cells and fluids like a permeation from the field of stillness. The body just loves this process!

CHAPTER 4

Peace and Autonomic Order

There is no peace without the nervous system being ordered and balanced. A constant state of distress from a world in survival mode often means this is a rare state. But as we know, when the brain and nervous system are regulated there is bliss. Finding this bliss is as simple as becoming aware of our internal state.

Understanding the biology of hyperarousal is also helpful. Hyperarousal means we are in autonomic overdrive. It involves some key parts of the central nervous system, along with a special endocrine organ – the adrenal glands – as well as the heart. So how do we come out of a hyperaroused state? The simplest way is to slow the heart down. It has a huge impact as its electrical system is the beat for the whole body. Every cell listens to it. Next is to help your adrenal glands. If you can reduce the production of cortisol into your bloodstream, then every cell in your body will be grateful. Lastly, convince the brain stem and limbic system to decelerate. In an adrenalized state, the brain stem and limbic system are hotspots that drive the body into high metabolic rates. Winding it down through felt sense awareness is the quickest way to physiologically calm down and bring yourself into a meditative state. Without a regulated system you can't truly meditate, so knowing signs of hyperarousal is very informative; otherwise, you will be blind to some obvious states of your body. Hyperarousal is a condition, a chronic state of long-term stress. Meditation takes place truly when the body is able to access its fluids, and it can't do that if it's freaking out. It's that simple. It's not a matter of sitting repeatedly in meditation but treating your body with a smart and knowing intention.

STRUCTURE OF THE AUTONOMIC NERVOUS SYSTEM

The autonomic nervous system, thus named because its response is automatic and involuntary, is built for survival. From very early in the embryonic stage, this unique part of the nervous system is constructed so that your body will have the necessary resources to respond to overwhelming situations, such as danger. Your response to danger needs to be reflex driven. It's not something you want to be thinking about, as immediate response is often what makes the difference between life and death. So this is a good reason for being 'wired up to fire up'. Fighting to defend yourself or fleeing to survive are built-in animal responses. When the situation is such that there is no escape or no possibility to fight, the response is to freeze. The body goes limp and you basically play dead. All of these responses can be seen in animal encounters. (Just search the Internet for fight-or-flight or freeze states and you'll find many examples of this.) In humans it can get complex. Our culture and big cerebral brains make the response come out in indirect ways that can interfere with the natural physical action and processing of these forces. The autonomic nervous system can therefore remain in chronic states of hyper- and hypoarousal, which ultimately leads to disease and low-energy conditions. Indeed, many health practitioners believe that unresolved autonomic states are behind all pathology.

The autonomics are organized into parasympathetic and sympathetic fibres. There are also autonomic centres in the brain stem and limbic system at the centre of the brain. Basically, they make the system go fast and go slow, processes that are quite complex in terms of the actual details. The fibres go to the organs of the body and run your physiology. That's why it's sometimes called the *visceral* nervous system. The heart is a perfect example of autonomic control mechanisms. The sympathetic nerves make the heart speed up and the parasympathetic nerves make it slow down. Between the two mechanisms, the heart's activity is controlled.

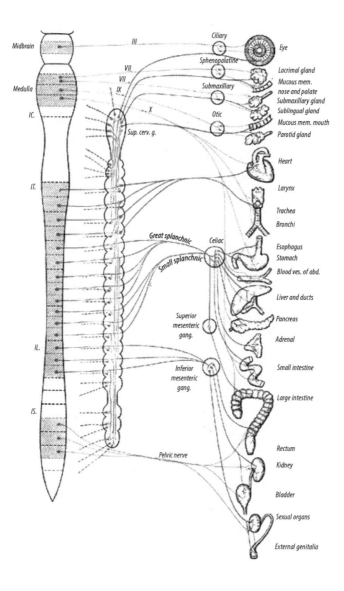

Figure 4.1 Structure of the autonomic nervous system

The neurology of the autonomic nervous system is extensive. On the whole, the sympathetic nervous system is concerned with mobilization and excitation and the parasympathetic nervous system with rest, recuperation and regeneration (Figure 4.1).

The big player in the parasympathetic nervous system is the vagus nerve, cranial nerve X. It is a huge nerve emerging bilaterally from the jugular foramen, hitching a ride alongside the major arteries and spreading to connect to all the major organs: heart, lungs, liver, pancreas, stomach, duodenum, small intestine and upper large intestine. This results in a massive amount of information being carried by one nerve.

The sympathetics are organized as a chain of nerve fibres that run down the length of the body alongside the spine and then branch out through nerve plexi into the organs of the chest and abdomen.

ASSESSING YOUR AUTONOMIC BALANCE

Here's how you can assess your autonomic balance:

- Signs of sympathetic activation – fight, flight or hyperarousal:

  ○ Faster respiration (to get oxygen in; over time, if this doesn't come back into balance, it can transform into tight, shallow breathing).

  ○ Quicker heart beat and pulse (to supply blood to the large muscles).

  ○ Increased blood pressure. (Both this and the above state can lead to high blood pressure symptoms and heart palpitations.)

  ○ Dilated pupils (to take in more light and information; this can lead to eyesight issues, particularly far-sightedness).

  ○ Pale skin colour (blood is diverted away from the periphery); long-term cold in extremities.

- ○ Increased sweating. (There is an expectation of heat being generated in the mobilization response, so sweating can be seen as a pre-emptive response to cool the body down.)

- ○ Cold, clammy skin (especially the hands, due to less blood in the periphery and increased sweating).

- ○ Decrease in digestive processes (including a dry mouth and contracted sphincters; this can lead to irritable bowel syndrome and other digestive disorders).

- ○ Tingling muscular tension; cramping and nervous tension.

- ○ Startle response; jumpiness and hypersensitivity.

- ○ Increased flexor tension (contracted body, especially the arms and legs which are subtly geared up for fighting [arms] and flighting [legs]).

Emotionally, sympathetic activation may be experienced as anxiety/panic, terror, aggression and everything happening too quickly, and it can be overwhelming.

- Signs of parasympathetic activation – freezing, dissociation or hypoarousal:

- ○ Tonic immobility (system can become limp and lacking in energy).

- ○ Numbing.

- ○ Dissociation (reduced felt sense awareness; can be a very frightening experience but can also be experienced as dreamy, floaty and pleasant – a place where you feel no pain).

- ○ Analgesia (this may be in the whole body, one side or one limb, or a part of one limb).

- ○ Inability to move a limb, dreams of not being able to move (one client called this 'sleep paralysis').

○ Inability to perceive the outline of the body (for example, hands or feet feeling too big, too small or too close or far away).

○ Inability to feel the skin as a sharply defined edge.

○ Sense of floating (which can be experienced as a whole-body sensation or felt as one side of the body being higher than the other when lying down).

○ Sense of disconnection (commonly from below the neck or diaphragm, or pelvis or feet).

○ Low muscle tone (hypermobility).

Emotionally, parasympathetic activation may be experienced as depression, withdrawal, feelings of unreality or not knowing and lethargy.

These are profound lists that can help you define how your system is in terms of retained trauma. Often we are a mix of both conditions, sympathetic and parasympathetic. Many people are caught up in these autonomic conditions, so if you are, too, sitting in meditation and accessing your deep health is going to be very difficult. Resolving arousal is key to deepening your meditation. Meditation needs autonomic balance to be able to access your full felt sense awareness, stillness and bliss. The energy taken up by maintaining the above states can be exhausting to the body's resources.

The process of healing involves becoming aware of these states. The body is holding difficult experiences it hasn't been able to release, and the coping mechanism is for the body to optimize its physiology and allow such experiences to move into the unconscious. The autonomic state then becomes chronic and embedded in your tissues and in the way your body functions. So opening up to felt sense awareness is a first step in acknowledging what is taking place in your body, state of mind, energy levels, digestion and breathing. All of this will improve with knowledge and finding the patterns and states that have become buried in your body. The body is desperate to resolve the effects of trauma, so any movement towards becoming conscious, through felt sense awareness, of what is being held in the body will bring the effects of trauma to the surface. As the body starts to access these states, you should expect to feel some emotional turbulence and mental fluctuations along with readjustments in your body's structure. Shaking and vibrating are common responses as the body discharges long-retained negative forces.

AUTONOMIC MEDITATIONS

Sympathetic nerves emerge from the thoracic spine and upper lumbar spine (it's called the thoracolumbar division of the autonomic nervous system) and form an interconnecting chain of ganglia on either side of the spine in front of the rib heads. The chain extends all the way down and joins with the ganglion impar in front of the coccyx. It looks like two long necklaces. It also extends up into the neck and head. The nerves form additional ganglia in the body cavities in front of the spine, called collateral ganglia, the most well known being the solar plexus. These nerves, plexi and ganglia innervate the gut and all the organs of the chest and abdomen. You can see them on the right in Figure 4.1.

Meditation: sympathetic nervous system

Using your awareness and Figure 4.1, try tuning into the sympathetic chain. Try to feel it running along either side of the vertebral column from the top of your neck to your coccyx. It has a powerful presence in the body, especially if it's hyperactive. When you are doing this you may also become aware of the visceral nerve network, including the collateral ganglia and plexi. Feel the quality and motion within the chain and its interactions with the organs. The brain stem and adrenal glands are other important hotspots of the sympathetic network. Frequently, there can be buzzy, dynamic, quick and hot qualities as you tune into these structures.

Meditation: parasympathetic nervous system

Now tune into the parasympathetic nervous system (also called the craniosacral division). This is principally carried by the vagus nerve, which originates in the brain stem. Start from its cranial nerve nuclei in the brain stem. See if you can imagine and follow the vagus nerve down through the cranial base and the neck into the thoracic chamber, and down through the diaphragm into the abdomen. This nerve is called the wanderer because it meanders through these two cavities and touches into all the organs via a series of plexi.

Notice, too, the pelvic nerves exiting from the sacrum into the pelvic cavity interacting with the pelvic viscera. So, unlike the sympathetic chain, the parasympathetics are more about the cranium and the sacrum – that is, the two ends of the vertebral axis. The action of the parasympathetic network is rest and recuperation. Try orienting to nervous activity in the parasympathetic centres at the base of the skull and in the pelvic bowl at the same time. How does this feel? Is it different from the sympathetic system? Perhaps you have a sense of the vagus nerve. Recent research is revealing how important a healthy vagus nerve is, not only for nervous system regulation but also immunity, inflammatory response and social interaction. It's important for regulating mood and reducing depression. It calms the heart and releases oxytocin.

Try being attuned to both the sympathetic/thoracolumbar division and the parasympathetic/craniosacral division systems together, and notice how the two interact.

Meditation: stories in the gut

The gut is our biggest internal organ, rich with both sympathetic and parasympathetic fibres.

Close your eyes. Be with a sense of your whole system. This is the integrated you. Now shift your perception to a sense of the whole of your digestive system from the mouth to the anus. Engage with the sense of softness, hollowness and fluidity in the active organs in the front of your body, especially in your belly but also connecting up to your mouth and down to your pelvis. Allow some time for your perceptions to settle, and try to keep a sense of your gut tube as part of your whole body.

Are there any words, phrases, images or emotions that fit to how your gut feels right now? What is your gut instinct of how you are right now? Explore your felt sense of what you are digesting and ruminating over in your gut, your body and your life.

Allow the possibility that these background sensations in your gut may reflect your visceral response to the important stories in your life. Do not try to change what you are feeling. Just be present: 'This is how my body is right now, this is how I am right now.' Try not to think in terms of good or bad, right or wrong.

When it feels right, slowly disengage the focus on your gut, connect to the weight of your body in the chair, hear the sounds in the room and slowly open your eyes. How do you feel?

CHAPTER 5

The Amazing Connective Tissue Body

Your body is mostly collagen. Collagen is the most versatile of molecules with over 20 different forms. You could think of it as the basic material of the body. It's like a fabric that weaves itself into different shapes and structures which then support all other tissues in the body. Collagen is the basis of connective tissues and it is intrinsic to bones, joints, ligaments, tendons, fascia and membranes. It's woven into pockets in which organs, muscles, nerves and vessels lie. In collagen, the body has a perfect molecule for the function of creating boundaries, skins and support structures.

Like all substances in the body, collagen has its own unique signature of sensation, texture and quality. Its most common feeling in the body is one of continuity. Not only does collagen wrap everything, but it also merges into other collagen structures to produce a continuum of fibrous material. This produces the feeling of wholeness and oneness in our felt sense awareness. One of the most common features of this is the feeling of wellness. It seems to be simply part of the experience. Living in the whole of your body is, after all, occupying your full space and is much more profound than living in part of your body or certain layers or aspects of it. The body has formed itself as a living entity and it works best when all parts and all systems come together in a coordinated response to the environment. Wholeness of mind comes along with this, too. Being partially embodied leads to fragmentation and finding mental clarity is not easy. When the body is supple and strong, and there is full body awareness, you are intelligent. Your mind simply reflects this, because it is supple, strong and aware; therefore, you can think straight and use the full force of the mind. This leads to emotional richness and stability. Above all, you become creative. This is our natural given right. Being creative means you live your life in an inspired and satisfying way. You actually know what interests you and what you want to do with your life. This is somebody who can cope with the rigours of life and who can be fulfilled.

All of this starts with the quality and texture of your connective tissues (Figure 5.1).

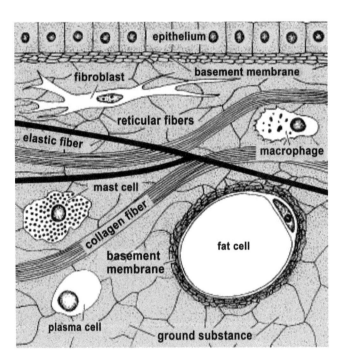

Figure 5.1 Connective tissues

These tissues surround everything in the body. They are the skins of all the body structure from the outer skin to the deep organ membranes to the covering of muscles and nerves. It's the ultimate support structure and is designed to be tough, elastic and fluid-like. The body is most intelligent when it can use its communication pathways of connective tissue. Blood vessels, nerves and lymphatics pass through the connective tissues to create a highway for circulation and transmission. If your connective tissues are in balance, the major systems of your body can be in homeostasis.

SKIN

The skin is the easiest layer of connective tissue to relate to in the body. It's what we see and touch, so it is the tissue with which we are most familiar. To track it with felt sense is easy.

Meditation: skin

Lie down on your back to do this exercise. Make sure that you are in a position you can hold for 15 minutes without moving the body. It's useful to place the back of your hands on the floor to your sides. Close your eyes and bring your awareness to your face. There's a strong sense of skin in your face. Notice the tone of your skin through the length and breadth of your face. Then follow this feeling into your forehead and down to your throat. There's a natural flow here that has to do with being particularly aware of this part of your skin, as it's the part we see most. From the forehead let your awareness track back over your scalp and into the back of the neck, and keep following the skin sensations out across the shoulders to your arms and hands. That's a natural flow of connectivity. Stay with that for a short while and notice differences in sensations for each arm and shoulder and both sides of the arms. Some sections may be more discernible and clearer in sensation, others may be much less clear and even some parts not really evident at all. The brain is more interested in certain parts of the skin than others, so it could have to do with that or maybe there has been an injury to the area.

Now follow the skin down the back of your torso and then down the front from the chest to the pubic arch. Simply notice the difference front and back. There should be a difference, but within that there may be areas that you can feel more obviously and areas less so. Again, some sections of the skin might feel not so present or clear. Sometimes the skin feels like it is either not there or blending into the space around you such that there is no clear definition or sense of boundary to it. This happens when the skin has been shocked or distressed.

Finally, let your awareness explore the legs and pelvis right down to the feet. The feet are often quite strong in presence, just like the hands, but parts of the legs might be less clear.

Now you can open up to the whole wrap of your skin. Be with the fullness of it.

Deep skins

The skin that is visible is the outermost skin of our body, but there are many more skins that wrap all the body structures. There are wrappings for muscles, bones, organs, nerves, blood vessels and joints. Everything has a skin. These deep skins have a variety of names – for example, fascia, periosteum, peritoneum, neurilemma, dura mater and synovial membrane, but they are essentially similar in that they are a collagen-based fabric that has strength and elasticity. It's an internal world of sliding surfaces so that everything can move freely around each other – muscles gliding over other muscles, internal organs sliding against each other. The important thing to understand is that all of these skins form an interconnecting network. There is both a layered system and a system where these tissues flow one into the next. There's a stream of connective tissues running mostly along the length of the body and the limbs, with some powerful exceptions in some key horizontal structures (see Chapter 6).

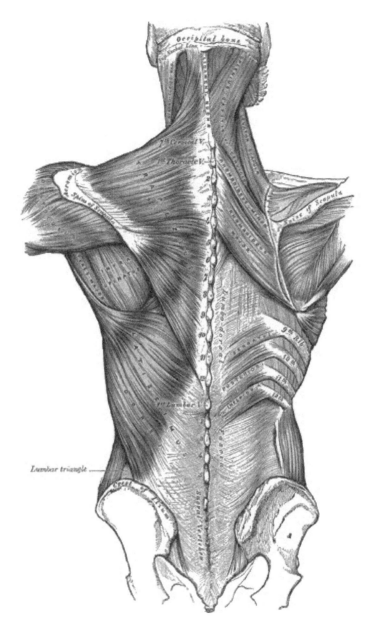

Figure 5.2 Fascia of the torso

BIOTENSEGRITY

Biotensegrity is an important theory of the body that everyone should know about. Biotensegrity stands for biological tension integrity. All structures, both naturally occurring and man-made, need to be in a state of balanced tension across all of their elements to be stable. Bridges and buildings are built on the tensegrity model, which is about the structure bearing its weight and strain across the whole structure, not just in one part of it. Sharing the load through a cross-connected structure evens out the load. Metal rods in cement creates a meshed construct not unlike the connective tissue fibres of the body. All living things are part of this phenomenon. Trees, animals, cells, the sea, planets and suns – all of them have this balanced-tension dynamic in common. The body attains this intermeshed system through its connective tissues. The body can be viewed as fibrous sheets that mesh together to form a continuum of fabric that is held in a balanced tension for optimal health.

The fabric of the body, however, can have a variety of different tensile energies. The body absorbs impacts and injuries throughout life which can leave their mark. Stress and strong emotional trauma can act exactly in the same way, leaving a patterned expression on the body fabric. This translates into hypertensile or hypotensile properties retained in the connective tissues. The body loses its balanced tension and becomes high or low in its tensile energy, resulting in an overall system reduction in balanced tension. The body therefore becomes less flexible, less mobile, less able to communicate across the whole and, most importantly, its ability to respond as a whole unit is reduced.

Biotensegrity is the quality of living structure that brings the local together with the whole. That's a huge perspective on the body and its response. It means that if we damage a joint, say, the knee, the ramifications of the injury will naturally include the whole body, because the knee does not exist in isolation. The holistic nature of the body means that the neck, cranium, upper limbs, the way you breathe, the way the heart beats and the balance of your endocrine system will all be affected. Some of these effects will be subtle and others much more gross and apparent. The body has been built as a whole unit of function, not a collection of parts. It will therefore respond with its wholeness to meet any stressor, be it internal or external. The nature of the connective tissue body is to absorb all experiences as a whole system, which allows the impact of the experience to be spread throughout the whole.

If there is a reduction in balanced tension in the body, there will be a similar response in the mind. The mind is no different from the body in this regard, it's biotensile. The most common response is for the body to become extremely tense. If this persists and becomes chronic, the body becomes less flexible. The mind follows suit and becomes more rigid. The body can also have too little tension. So flaccidity predominates, which weakens the posture and brings about low-energy states. As described above, the mind follows the body and becomes low in energy, leading to poor concentration and a lack of clear rational thinking. If these biotensile energies mount up over the years through a series of traumatic events, the mind and the body will become stagnant. You are how you move, and you move from your biotensile energy. Fortunately, you can work with this. The first thing is to recognize your tensile health. We all have a biotensegrity body that is trying its best to compensate and optimize. Recognizing the amazing ability your body has to do that means you need to come into awareness of your whole tensile field. There is a power of health that can be accessed within that is often severely repressed.

The other thing to do is to be able to map your tensile body with felt sense awareness so that you are in a much more conscious relationship to it. That makes a huge difference. It means you are present to how your body actually is, rather than in a foggy relationship to it. The body loves presence, it thrives on it. The power of presence will bring cells and structures into a new consciousness and energy, and it will revive the body's ability to adjust and realign from within.

Meditation: biotensegrity

Initially try this meditation standing. Try standing with ease. Inspect your body for any unnecessary strains in your posture. Consciously allow them to dissolve and watch your body re-posture automatically. Use Figure 5.3 to bring you into the matrix of your tensile body. It's important that you don't lose the sense of the whole as in that resides your maximum health expression. Be interested in the longitudinal flow of tissues that runs from your feet to your head via your pelvis and spine. When you sense it, there is a feeling of streaming of tissues. This is an awareness of your connective tissue system. Notice, too, the transverse or horizontal tissue flows across the body.

Now answer these questions for yourself:

- Do I feel tense?

- Are there some areas that feel constricted?

- Is there discomfort?

- Are there emotional feelings?

Ask your body these questions and it will let you know the answer through feeling tones. Stay with the interconnectedness of the body. All you need to do is simply acknowledge how things are and the body's intelligence will generate automatic shifts in structural alignment. Your part in it is becoming skilled at holding the whole with the local detail through your conscious awareness. Then there is a healing. The biotensegrity of the body is highly mutable and can change dynamically. All it needs is attention and understanding. You are, in effect, counselling your physiology.

Now continue the exercise in a sitting position and notice how your structure and biotensegrity are consistent when sitting and standing. The highlighting of posture and tensile energy of the whole body when standing elucidates your tensile body when you sit, and you can sit with a greater clarity.

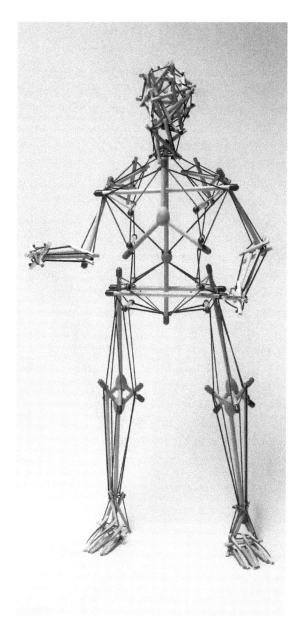

Figure 5.3 Biotensegrity man

CONNECTIVE TISSUE SYSTEM: THE BIGGEST SENSORY ORGAN

Our nervous systems are organized into input and output from and to the central nervous system of the brain and spinal cord. The output has to do with body movement, which on the whole is voluntary. It's called our motor nervous system because it drives motion and is all about the nervous system's relationship to muscles. The input aspect is our sensory nervous system and is about sensory information coming into the brain and spinal cord from our special and general senses. The special senses are driven by specialized cranial nerves in the head. So the senses of sight, smell, hearing, taste and touch constitute the special senses and give rise to a lot of information about our environment. We are powerfully dominated by these senses; however, the sensory information coming from what is called the general senses dwarfs all of these senses. The general senses come from sensory receptors located throughout the connective tissue body and therefore make your connective tissue system your biggest sensory organ. Being in felt sense relationship to it means you are in relationship to a highly refined feeling of how your body is and how your environment feels. So if there is disruption in your connective tissue system, there may well be a reduction in sensory information about that area and an overall reduction in your sensitivity. Reorganization of your connective tissue system is therefore key to becoming more sensitive.

Meditation: sensory awareness

Come into awareness of your whole body. Now be interested in the relationship between the periphery and the core of your body. The sensory flow into the core of the body is a factor of 100 times greater than the motor flow out of the core. So if you attune to your nervous flows into and out of the core, the first thing you should feel is an electrostatic sensory flow into the spinal cord and up to the brain coming in from all parts of the body. This can take a few attempts to notice the feeling of nervous impulse. Know that nervous receptors reside within your connective tissues as well as offer passage for nerve fibres. Notice how smooth the flow is from different parts of your body.

Let's take each limb in turn. Starting with your right arm, tune into the tensile energy of your arm at the same time as you feel the sensory nervous tone flowing into the body. Now consciously relax your arm from your fingers to the palm to the wrist and forearm. Let go of weight into your elbow and shoulder joints. Acknowledge the arms as an extension of the chest and not as something separate. Let the chest and arms blend together. As the body is responding to this, you will notice a change in the sensory nervous flow, in both its quality and quantity. Now repeat the same process for the other arm and both legs. The whole process should take 5 minutes for each limb. This is a great way to join up your body and create a continuity across all the connective tissues and consequent increase in sensory flow. The brain loves this as do all body structures. A sensitive body system is being created that leads to greater body awareness and a literal increase in sensitivity.

Your body receptors monitor for changes in motion, temperature and pressure. At the end of the meditation, if you open up to all of the layers of your connective tissue body and imagine the surface area of this being so great that you are like a satellite dish of receptors to both your internal landscape and the external environment, you will come into the power of your amazing connective tissue sensorium.

LIVING MEMBRANOUS BODY

The body is highly membranous. Membranes offer protection for key structures such as the heart, brain and gut. The word membrane comes from a Latin etymology meaning parchment. So membranes are thin, sheet-like connective tissues. In health they offer sliding surfaces and communication pathways for blood, nerves and lymph, but overall they offer protection and tensegrity for what lies within the body. All too often these membranes have powerful holding patterns within them that are expressed as tissues strains. Connective tissue strains produce microscopic reorganization of collagen molecules into patterns of knotted fibres. This creates a thickening in the membrane structure that makes it less mobile and dehydrated, as fluids are less able to move freely when tissues are constrained.

These membranes hold powerful forces which, when released, generate great changes across whole sections of the body. The pericardium, for example, can generate so much contraction that it can hold the whole ribcage in its grip and, when released, allows the whole ribcage, spine and diaphragm to let go, allowing breathing to deepen. So appreciating the power of membranes within your body is a big insight into how we can contract, and that contraction is not just about muscles (Figure 5.4).

There are seven major membranes of the body: the skin, pericardium, pleura (two), peritoneum, synovial membranes and dura mater. Each membrane creates an internal space for the function of organ systems and provides a boundary for the chemistry and gross movement of the structures within them. That makes these membranes highly significant in the body. In effect, they are the real cavities of the body. Their state of health is key to how the organ systems function and therefore how *you* function. They are highly sensory. Membranes have many receptors in them that can give rise to a deep and unique state of internal awareness. To be in relationship to your membranes means you are in contact with your primal skins.

Membranes all communicate with each other. There's a membranous conversation running in our bodies that is beyond the simple connectivity of their structures. They resonate. So health or strain in one membrane has an effect on all the others. Something about membranes and their function of protection makes them highly vulnerable to emotional stress. Commonly these membranes contain difficult unresolved experiences that invidiously create disruption. Other than the skin, all the other membranes lie deep in the body, so to bring them into balanced membranous tension is one of the best things you can do for your body. The ramifications of this can bring about a shift in breathing, remodelling of posture, new neuroendocrine balance and clarity of thought, all leading to further embodiment.

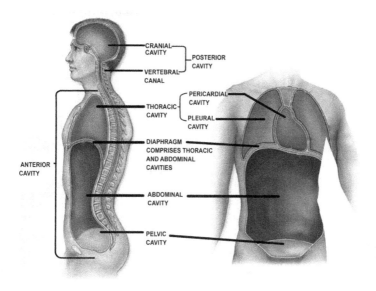

Figure 5.4 Body cavities and membranes

Meditation: pericardium

Knowing your structural detail is so profound and allows you to understand your body with much greater depth. The pericardium (Figure 5.5) is the heart's protector. It needs to be tough but pliable in order to accommodate the strong motion of the heart but at the same time offer a firm boundary to it. Knowing the attachments of the pericardium is important because these are its anchors for motion and stability. Even though the pericardium is a thin-layered connective tissue, it is tough and fibrous and can exert strong pulls into its attachments when strained.

Sitting comfortably, let's follow the felt sense of the pericardium. As always, open up to the whole. Open up to the whole connective tissue body and stay with an awareness of it throughout the meditation so that you are not overly focused on the pericardium. All membranes are in relationship to the whole connective tissue system. They are part of its continuity, so having an awareness that mirrors that continuity is deeply healing to the body. It provides perspective when perspective has been lost.

Feel your way into the pericardium. Try to feel its membranous tension. Does it feel at ease or tense? When it's tense, it can be confused with tension in the ribs or diaphragm. Now track its attachments. The biggest one is into the diaphragm itself. The diaphragm and pericardium have grown up together. They originated in the early embryonic period in close proximity to each other and have been connected since your earliest moments of life in utero. So there is no surprise that there is a close bond between them. The heart sits in the pericardium, which is bonded with the centre of the diaphragm. How does this feel? The pericardium has two attachments to the sternum: one at the front and one onto the spine at the back. Now shift to the two attachments into the sternum, the centre of the ribcage. How does this feel? Now shift to the attachment into the spine at the back at T3/4 between your shoulder blades. Once again, how does this feel? Finally, there are numerous softer lines of attachment moving upwards into the throat, jaw and cranial base. How does that feel? In the exploration you may have found some attachments to be very tight and constrained, and others not so. Repeating the meditation with the relationship to the whole continuity and health of the connective tissue body and the pericardium and its particular tension patterns is a wonderful way of offering perspective to your body structures that will lead to dissolution of tension and processing of any structural or emotional patterns.

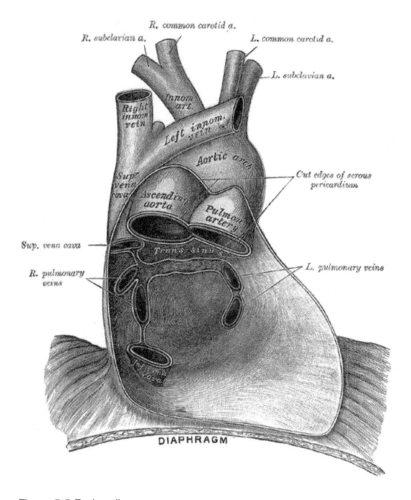

Figure 5.5 Pericardium

CHAPTER 6

Diaphragmatic Wholeness

Your body is whole. It is one unit of function that is based on cell communication. The body has been formed from an original axis of growth, so it is mostly longitudinal but also horizontal. There are key horizontal structures that divide you into sections (Figure 6.1). Chief of these sections is your respiratory diaphragm. This is the biggest structure in the body in terms of the extent and spread of tissue. It's like an internal parachute. Everything in the body, therefore, is affected by it. The word diaphragm means interface between spaces, and that is exactly what it is. It is the interface between your chest and abdominal cavities. It is also a unique structure in that it is both voluntarily and involuntarily controlled by us. There's nothing quite like it in the body.

Here are some of the major diaphragms of the body:

- soles of the feet

- pelvic floor

- respiratory diaphragm

- shoulder girdle

- cranial base

- tentorium cerebelli

- roof of the mouth

- crown of the head.

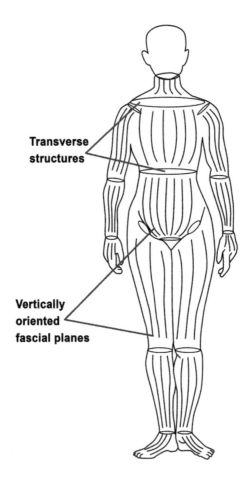

Figure 6.1 Longitudinal fascia and transverse structures

THE NATURE OF DIAPHRAGMS

The diaphragms are a mix of different structures that all have the common ground of being transverse or horizontal. The soles of the feet are mostly constructed of the plantar fascia, which is a long series of banded connective tissues. They have a profound effect on your whole body but in particular the other diaphragms. If your feet are relaxed, then your whole body is relaxed. If they are tight and constricted, then other diaphragms tighten in response. Tension requires lots of energy to maintain, and as whole regions of the body dissolve constrictions, the body has more energy.

The pelvic floor is a mixture of muscles that allow for the passage of the urogenital and gut systems. Like the feet, the structures here can be defining in the whole body's health. Often when there is stress, anxiety or fear, the muscles of the pelvic floor become tight and affect pelvic balance and movement of the legs. This can disrupt postural alignment.

The shoulder girdle is a combination of muscles, bones and joints that overall act as a cross-structure for the upper body to pivot around. Tension here is so common. Tight necks and shoulders have spawned an industry of bodyworkers striving to relieve tension build-up in these areas. Balance in this area can be profound and relieve the body of deep tensions.

The thoracic inlet is a term for the centre of the shoulder girdle around the clavicle, first rib and lower neck. It's an area that is mainly involved in the passage of blood, air and food, so it contains a lot of different kinds of tubes. The more at rest and expanded this section of the body becomes, the easier the flow will be.

The cranial base is a bony structure on which the brain sits and with which the spine articulates. Even though it is bone and joint in nature, it still acts as a diaphragm. Tension in the jaw and upper neck have significant effects on the cranial base. Relaxing your cranial base could be one of the most relieving things you can do in your body. You breathing will be changed by it, your digestion will improve and the way you move, as well as your posture, will be affected. The cranial base is significant. Just above it and involved in it is a big membrane called the tentorium cerebelli (literally tent of the cerebellum). It holds the cranial base together and helps support the brain. It is naturally elastic and acts as a trampoline for the brain. Membranous tension here restricts the cranial base and creates tension throughout the cranium.

Lastly, let's look at the crown of the head, which is a curved hemispheric structure that includes bone and membrane. It reflects powerfully with the pelvic floor, so much so that one could say they are mirror images of each other. For example, often headaches originate from tension in the pelvic floor, or pelvic floor tensions can be resolved when the crown or the cranial vault softens. Bones can relax within themselves. They are, after all, made of collagen fibres like ligaments, tendons and fascia.

The theory of biotensegrity is life changing. It describes how your body is a matrix of fibres that acts like a building. In order to maintain its strength and integrity, the body requires a tensile energy that brings all the tissues into a continuity of relationship. The body is a knit of fibres that creates a three-dimensional network seeking balanced tone. Tensile energy in the body is both longitudinal and horizontal, and the diaphragms of the body are key to optimal tensile energy.

When healthy, our tissues have a natural elasticity like springy trampolines that act as membranous energy plates. When they are all in communication with each other, there is a real connection throughout the body and the major systems can move and interact. Nerves, vessels and lymphatics all pass through these structures on their way to another section of the body. When we become distressed or feel threatened, we start to tighten these diaphragms as part of the process of flight or fight. We can also use these diaphragms to fragment ourselves when we become overwhelmed and can't cope. This allows us to reduce our presence by compartmentalizing the body. It's a clever mechanism that allows us to carry on through difficulties; however, other difficulties begin to arise when we don't recover from this fragmented state. When this fragmented stage continues, the system becomes static, which commonly leads to contraction, exhaustion and anxiety.

Optimal health is about a dynamic system rather than a static, fragmented one. Becoming aware of tension in the transverse structures is the first step to regaining a dynamic system and returning to a balanced state.

Meditation: respiratory diaphragm

Sitting comfortably, bring the palm of your hand to the bottom of your sternum (half on the bony sternum and half into the soft tissue of the solar plexus). Take the back of your other hand and place it onto the curve of your lower back. Between your hands is the whole diaphragm, which attaches to your sternum and inserts into your ribs and the middle of the lumbar curve of the spinal column. If you move your hand at the front down by a hand width, you will notice that you have lost the sense of something continuous between your hands. Bring it back up and open your awareness to the wholeness of the body. Spend a couple of minutes doing this. It's an interesting feeling when you allow all the other parts of the body to come into relationship with the diaphragm. It may take a few meditations to truly be able to do this.

The second part to this meditation is to follow the movement of your diaphragm between your hands as it shifts from inhalation to exhalation, without trying to change it in any way. You are being a true observer of your own breathing. Simply notice how your diaphragm generates an in breath and an out breath.

The action of the diaphragm in health accounts for 70% of your breathing, so it's a mighty movement in the body. Now let go of the hands and simply follow it with your awareness. You are listening to the movement of your diaphragm at the centre of your whole body.

The third part is to notice how much of the body is moving in response to the action of the diaphragm. The simplest things to notice are the movement of your chest and abdomen, but also check out the shift in shape and position of your vertebral column, including the tilt and shift of your head.

Finally, follow any response in the legs and arms. At first, these responses may not be present, but the more you give your breath attention with this meditation, the more all the strands of the body start to participate. When breathing is whole-body, the most amazing energy is generated from it.

This meditation is designed to last 10 minutes. For the last few minutes, simply let go of any focus on your breath and let your mind rest.

Meditation: transverse diaphragms

This exercise is best to do standing. Start with your lowest diaphragm. Bring your awareness to your feet. Notice the tops of the feet and the soles of the feet. They feel quite different, and this will enable you to get a sense of the volume and depth of your feet. The sole of the foot is in touch with the floor, which gives you a sense of contact and pressure into the soles.

Notice the different feeling between both feet. You might not be able to put it into words, but there's a qualitative difference between them. Follow what happens when you ask your body to relax into your feet. Let the feet soften and spread. This will bring you into a fuller sense of the soles of the feet. Notice if there is any tension along the length of the soles. Invite your soles to relax into the floor and follow what happens not just in the feet but through the whole body. You might notice other parts of the body responding to this.

Stay with the sense of wholeness and now move your awareness to your pelvic floor. Run through a similar process here. Initially notice how the area feels between the bottom of your sacrum and coccyx at the back and your pubic arch at the front. Then notice how it feels across from hip to hip. As you become aware of sensations, there will be details of how it feels. Let the whole area consciously relax and follow the effects through the pelvis down the legs to the feet, and notice if any of the other diaphragms change in response.

Shift your awareness again, this time to the respiratory diaphragm. If you put your hand on the bottom of your breast bone/sternum and the back of the other hand behind the front hand and down a half hand width, you will have the diaphragm between your hands. If you move both hands higher, the sense of connection disappears; the same thing happens if you move them lower. Coming back to the first position, you should feel the connection again, this time perhaps more vividly. The respiratory diaphragm is the master transverse diaphragm. Let your diaphragm soften and relax into your hands and follow the change in your whole body as it does.

Moving your awareness to your shoulders and thoracic inlet, notice the felt sense the area generates. If you listen to that part of the body in relationship to the other diaphragms you've connected with previously, it will help create a perspective. The body likes nothing more than perspective. It provides an opportunity to relate across the whole and harness the full health and intelligence of your body. Just creating that attention will bring about a reorganization of the area, which can be felt as a movement of tissues and fluids.

Follow the same process for the cranial base and the tentorium, and then for the crown of the head. Stay neutral in your awareness of the body and be a curious witness to how your body responds.

Now sit comfortably in a meditation posture and start by opening up to a relationship to all the diaphragms within the whole of your body. Having gone through the standing awareness exercise, the diaphragms should come into your awareness easily. Have an intention to stay in conscious relationship with them for 5 minutes and listen to the response. Then let go of the intention and be neutral to any particulars, sitting and watching the body in a diaphragmatic wholeness.

CHAPTER 7

Breath and Life

Breathing is the most profound and affecting movement in the body. It can also be the most disrupted. Research suggests that 80% of people breathe poorly. To take in and give out air is one of the basic functions of life, so it's tragic that so many of us struggle around it. It's like we are fighting to stay alive. It's phenomenal that there is also such a lack of understanding of how breathing actually occurs. When asked, people have to pause and think about how they breathe before they can answer.

There's a wonderful exercise that, in an instant, will bring about both an increased awareness of, and a positive change in, the breathing process.

Meditation: breathing

Simply start by becoming aware of your breathing and of the felt sense of it. Just observe your body while you breathe without trying to change your breath. Make sure you don't change your breath consciously. Just be with the sensation of it, not the idea or thought of it. Follow the movements of breathing. Notice how it naturally starts to change and deepen. It might take a couple of minutes. Give your body a chance to find its natural, unencumbered breath. There's a biological, optimized breath that wants to emerge; it only needs the right attention and permission to arise. In time, it can establish itself so that the physiology of the body is regulated and the mind is calm.

Now purposefully start thinking of something in your life. This will shift you to a mental space. Observe what happens to your breath. Observe, too, what happens when you think of something stressful.

The lungs, ribcage, diaphragm and a whole host of muscles are designed to create a synchronized movement of the whole body to achieve a breath cycle. It's not something that happens just in the chest. The whole body is involved in full breathing. When it's not fully involved, there's a reduction in motion and energy as well as a change in posture. So breathing as inclusively as possible is an optimal practice that will lead to a dynamic homeostasis of the body.

Bringing back the full motion of breath is vital. That's why so many spiritual and exercise traditions hold it to be so important. Look at yoga, chi kung and Pilates. Focus on the breath is the foundation of these practices. How you breathe is one of the biggest effectors of your state of mind, energy levels and emotions. Connecting with the breath has long been considered a path to spiritual enlightenment.

Your breath supplies cells with oxygen, so if your breathing is compromised, your cells get starved of oxygen and, as a consequence, your health is diminished. What stops the breathing process from happening optimally? Babies are really good breathers. We have all been babies, so life started with a deep belly breathing that was totally whole-bodied. That's the natural expression of the breath.

So the real questions is, how do we lose the baby state of being? Life comes along and you experience difficult events with which you need to deal. One of our primal responses to threat is to gear up for defence or escape. The biology of trauma affects the breath very powerfully. Gearing up involves the breath quickening so that you are bringing more oxygen into your body for short-term consumption. This means you are panting. The body needs to recover from this response, but if the threatening event was too difficult or overwhelming, the body doesn't get this chance and the state of hyperarousal stays in the system. Over time, it manifests as shallow breath and a tight ribcage. The breathing mechanism becomes disordered. The breathing muscles are not just part of the ribcage but also extend into the shoulders and the neck area and down into the abdomen. Those muscles can get caught up with this and become tight. So the classic profile is shallow breath, tight ribcage, shoulder and neck tensions, and holding in the abdominal muscles. Obviously, this will affect your spine and limbs, plus all the other systems of the body: circulatory (high blood pressure), nervous (hyperactivity), joints (poor posture and pain) and endocrine (swings in levels of hormones). If that sounds familiar, you are suffering from poor breathing, which underlies many disease symptoms.

NATURAL, WHOLE-BODY BREATHING

Breathing is about bringing oxygen into your cells. It's also about being in relationship with your environment. We are taking in air from around us and giving it back out. This flux means we are constantly exchanging with the world around us. We are totally part of it, even though a lot of the time it can feel like we are separate. Feeling separate is the most incredible deception. How can we possibly be separate from our environment when we are breathing in the world around us all the time? Re-establishing this connection can be the most powerful thing we do. It's all about perception and awareness, and natural, whole-body breathing is the foundation.

Sitting still and following your breath is remarkably simple and illuminating. When we start to follow the ebb and flow of air moving into and out of our lungs, and into and out of our cells, the body begins to feel highly energized and there is an arising bliss in the experience. Following your breath means observing how your body is going about breathing without interfering. So if you become the silent, non-acting observer of your body, you will quickly feel the movements of your breath. Over time, we normalize to how things feel and then they don't seem unusual anymore. The body just feels how it always felt. But if you really listen, you can start to appreciate how the body might be functioning. Levels of tension are quite discernible as are patterns of ease and strain. The other factor is lack or ease of motion. So you can feel how your breath is in terms of ease and motion. How much motion is there? How much ease is there? It can get quite complex. Parts of the breathing process can be free and other parts caught up.

It's not possible to meditate when you can't breathe properly. Your body is not in homeostatic balance until breathing is smooth and easy. The brain and your mental process is then able to become ordered. Homeostatic balance is the prerequisite for meditation. Once this is available, your mind can become calm, and the mind becoming calm is the body becoming calm. The mind will follow the body.

There's a simple way of encouraging your system to free up around your breathing. The trick is to follow all the strands of your breath right out to all parts of your body. That way you can feel the connection to the breath, and it will start a thawing of the body to a state of liquid. Then the breath becomes original. You start to breathe how you are meant to breathe and how you did when you were a baby. So let's start to change our breathing through the experiential awareness exercises below.

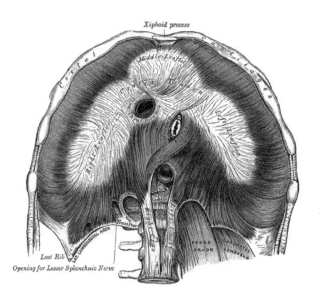

Figure 7.1 Diaphragm

Meditation: posture and breathing

Standing on two legs is such an amazing phenomenon. As a species we've forgotten this because it is so familiar. The brain and musculoskeletal system does the most remarkable juggling act to make it happen. The key to standing well is your breath.

Stand for a few minutes and experiment with your breathing. Slow it down and allow it to become softer and more full. Notice how your posture is changed by it. Then think of something stressful and follow the shift in your alignment. Now think of something that makes you happy. Once again, notice how your posture is changed by it. Next try standing and opening up to the body's intelligence. Let your body take over your breathing and let it change your posture from within. Try to follow the naturalness of the body, and stand for 5 minutes while this process continues.

It's fascinating watching what your body does given the chance to reorder itself. The body has the capability to adjust and reform itself at minute levels. If you practise this meditation, you will notice more permanent changes in your posture and breathing as the new form becomes embedded in your physiology.

Meditation: breathing and your spine

Bring your awareness to your chest and feel the way your ribcage moves. You can shift your awareness in a way that is following the movement of the ribcage as a whole. It feels like your awareness is spread throughout all of the ribs from front to back of the body. As you follow the motion, notice how the ribcage pivots around the rib joints along the spinal column. That's where the joint movements for the ribcage originate. It provides a different sense of your breathing and a feeling that breathing happens from the back of the body as well as the front. Most of our attention is oriented to the front of the body and the chest when we think of breathing. Stay with the movements but expand your awareness now to the length of your spine from the sacrum and coccyx at the back of your pelvis and the top of the spine into the cranium. What kinds of movements can you feel along your spinal column as you inhale and exhale?

Are parts of the spine moving in participation or not? Now just stay with following this, and you will find that the spine and the ribcage breathing start to move as a whole unit rather than only some parts moving together. This allows your breath to become more holistic.

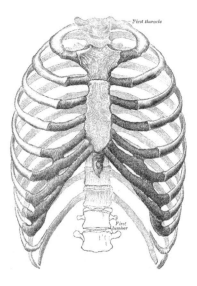

Figure 7.2 Ribcage

Meditation: breathing and euphoria

Sit and let the body become still and then come into the sensations of your breathing and follow the movements of breath for a couple of minutes. Do this with your eyes closed. Then, as you open your eyes, open up your awareness to the space around your body. Now be interested in the movement of air around you into and out of your lungs. Stay with this for a minute and notice changes in how your body feels. Now open up to the whole space of the room you are in and follow your breathing now for a couple of minutes. The feelings and sensations in your body will have changed, as you are coming into a deeper connection with the environmental dimension of breathing. Keep your eyes open with a soft peripheral vision. Lastly, open up to the whole of the environment that you and all of us are part of and notice the shift in your body tone.

CHAPTER 8

Inner Volume and Depth

There's a richness of body volume that starts to emerge when you are in a deeper felt sense awareness. It's fascinating reading about people's internal sense of their body shapes. When people are asked to draw how they think they appear to others, there can be a strong difference between that and the externally observed reality. It's the same with the internal sense. The relationship to the reality of the body can be quite different to the internal sense and interpretation of the interior. Most of this comes through interoception (sensitivity to stimuli originating inside of the body), which produces a flow of information of internal spaces, movement of viscera, density, flow of blood and nerves, and tensile energy.

Our bodies occupy space. We take up room through our body mass, which has a unique composition and dimensions of depth, length and width. To appreciate our volume is enriching to our felt sense. Often we can feel two-dimensional as our bodies deal with stress and trauma. The body can also feel everything on the outside with a very reduced sense of internal landscape. This is consistent with the body being locked into looking out through the special senses and being out of relationship with the general senses that bring information about volume and deep body sensing.

When we engage with our three-dimensional body we feel our length more keenly. We are mostly long creatures. If we feel our length and width, we feel gravity and there is a strength to that. If we feel our depth, we feel our interior. Being internalized and introspective comes with that. If you feel your depth, you are deep!

All of this can be increased through practice. The first thing to begin with is your relationship to the big internal spaces of the cavities. They define our internal sense most dramatically. Once you have the detail of this, you can start to appreciate the contents of the cavities.

There are three major cavities in the body: craniospinal, thoracic and abdominal. Each one of them represents different functions. The craniospinal cavity houses the central nervous system and is therefore a fluid–electrical phenomenon. The thoracic cavity is about the process of breathing and bringing air and blood into relationship. The abdominal cavity is about digestion. A relationship to each cavity therefore brings you into closer relationship with these fields of function and your major systems. The quality and motion of each cavity is unique. The dimensions of the space are unique, too. Developing an enriched sensory awareness of your cavities gives you a sense of your three-dimensionality, which creates a much deeper embodiment and gives rise to a more intimate connection to the forces of life and health within your system.

AWARENESS IN THE THREE CAVITIES
Meditation: opening to length, depth and width

Stand for this meditation. Invite a whole-body awareness into your perception. Now connect to the Cartesian axes. Top/bottom is the first axis. It brings you into your length as well as the space above and below you. Be interested in the top of your cranium and the soles of the feet as starting points into body length. Front/back is the next axis. Front space and back space create a feeling of depth. The space behind us is often quite disconnected initially. We are more commonly connected with the space in front of us. So repeat this section until a sense of it starts to arise. Finally, be interested in the spaces to the left and right as well as the flanks of the body.

This opens up our width and brings us into connection with the sides of the body. The flanks are places that are not prominent in our awareness, so teasing this out of our felt sense can produce an unusual perceptual field. Now be with all the dimensions at the same time and notice how they all start to blend into a smooth three-dimensional perception then as you continue into one whole dimension.

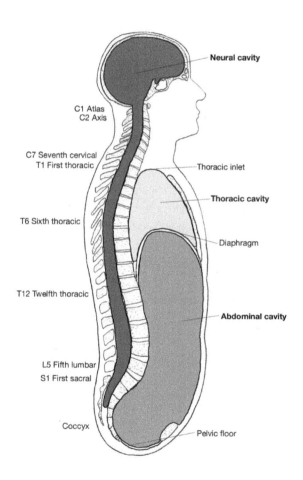

Figure 8.1 Body cavities

Meditation: awareness of three cavities

Sit for this meditation. Come into whole-body awareness and your three-dimensionality. Be interested in the felt sense of your lower torso. Track the extent of the lower cavity with your attention. Use Figure 8.1 to help with this. Start with your pelvic floor. There might be a whole mix of feelings and sensations. It could also feel quite numb or disconnected. With practice this can change.

Now follow the feeling up your abdominal wall from your pelvis to the edge of your ribs. This is the front wall of the cavity. At the top of the cavity is your diaphragm at the level of the lowest point of your breastplate or sternum. This is a flat structure that is domed. Follow the dome of it as it slopes off into the back wall of the abdomen and the vertebral column. Open up to the whole cavity. Notice that the lower part of the cavity is bony pelvis and the front is soft tissue. The cavity is an actual space that is defined by these structures and holds the lower organs of the torso. The cavity is like an inner cave (the word has the same derivation). Use this cavity as a place from which to listen. Now open up to the space around you and feel how it is in relationship to the abdominal cavity. Try to be equally aware of the internal and external spaces. Stay with it for a few minutes.

Repeat the same process for the thoracic cavity. Track the borders of the cavity using Figure 8.1. The structure here is quite different from the abdominal cavity. Its boundary is the ribcage. The shoulder girdle is at the top and the diaphragm is at the bottom. It's a much smaller cavity and the physiology is quite different. Once you have a sense of the cavity as an internal space, open up a state of balanced awareness with the space around you. A different kind of information comes to you about your environment. Notice if you feel more or less connected to this cavity.

Repeat the same process for the craniospinal cavity. This is in reality one cavity. Start with feeling the cranial aspect of this. This cavity is an exoskeleton. Come into sensation of your cranial bones. Invite a connection to the internal space of the neurocranium and follow this space with your awareness down the length of your vertebral column to your sacrum. The shape of this cavity is quite different from that of the other two. It also contains a totally different physiology. Open up the space around you and listen from this internal cavity. Again, notice the differences as compared with the other two cavities and, using your felt sense, notice how well you are in relationship to it.

Finally, open back up to your thoracic cavity and your abdominal cavity, so that you are highly aware of each cavity. At your first attempt this may not be possible. Maintain an intention towards this for a few minutes, and then relax. Don't keep up the focus. Something special starts to occur when you can generate the following:

- an equal felt sense awareness of each cavity

- an equal felt sense awareness of all three cavities simultaneously

- a spacious internal relationship with your body

- feeling capacity with regard to your environment that creates a state of balanced awareness.

CHAPTER 9

Fluid Body and Bliss

We all know that our bodies are composed of 75% water, similar to the make-up of the Earth's surface (at about 70% water and 30% land). Our bodies are reflective of this, being mostly salt water. The thing we call structure is merely a collection of salty fluid cells.

The body has 100 trillion cells in a fluid connective tissue matrix. Each cell has a membranous skin that is the container for the inner cytoplasmic fluid. Like the body as a whole, the cell, too, is mostly fluid with some structure. Our natural state, therefore, is the liquid state. The body is a fluid body, so it's strange that we feel solid. In fact, it's a *miracle* that we feel solid. There is no scientific explanation for how we create solidity out of so much water. We are fluid entities that appear to be solid. We emerge out of a fluid state as embryos and develop in a fluid sac, and then create enough solidity to be able to walk upright. Then, over time, we get used to this and think of ourselves as solid and structural. We indeed do have structure. The body has a definite anatomy to it. But all of it has emerged from a fluid body that we have forgotten and that still exists within us. Our orientation to a materialistic universe is born of this amnesia, so our minds have become solid and structural when, in fact, they also are fluid.

SOLID STATE

The stress and strain of life, along with distressing events, hold us in a contracted state. This keeps us away from the underlying fluidity. When there is ease in the body, you can drop below the surface to the fluids within it. This is what happens when you go on holiday and relax. Your body feels softer and more fluid-like and you feel happy. Being fluid and being happy are closely linked. Your natural state is to live in your fluids, so being separated from the experience is bad for your health.

You can learn to distinguish the solid and fluid states in your body. When the body finds its fluids, the mind becomes fluid too and there is a profound shift in perception. A sense of expansiveness and softness comes to you and the mind becomes more subtle. There are not so many concrete thoughts in this state, as it's more of an ideation state. The fluids are also a carrier of happiness. There's an inherent state of bliss as you morph from the solid to the liquid state. The edges of the body don't seem so defined. It feels like you flow with the environment rather than being separate from it.

FLUID-BODY RESONANCE

There's something else about the fluid body: it resonates with other fluid bodies. It's the nature of fluid. So you find that being in this state brings about a natural empathy towards others and you can literally sense another's body. The fluid state opens up an ability to be in deep communion with other fluid beings, that is, all other humans and all creatures, as we are all modelled on the same principle. This is what happens when we fall in love. We shift to our fluid bodies and merge with another person. That's what brings so much joy and energy. Fluid bodies like merging. When we don't merge, we become separate and unhappy.

Babies and children are wonderful examples of being in the fluid body. That's why we feel such an affinity with them – they are soft and supple, and we resonate with their fluids.

Humans experience powerful relationships to bodies of water. Going to the seaside and swimming or floating in the sea brings our bodies into a fluid state, and there's a balancing of our systems that brings our heart rate down, hypertension lowers, breathing slows and we come into a more dynamic connection with our body's most significant element. When we swim or float in the sea, we are like one of our cells: inside we are salt water and outside we are moving in salt water, just like our intra- and extracellular fluid volumes.

We have a lot of fluid within us. For an average weight of 60 kilograms, the body has 42 litres (nearly 9 gallons) of fluid. Two thirds of it is within cells, and most of the rest is between cells in the interstitial spaces. (Blood plasma is only 10% of our entire fluid body.)

Below are a series of felt sense awareness exercises that will open up this inner relationship and bring you into contact with your fluid state, your *true* state.

Meditation: fluid body

Sitting in a chair, become aware of your whole body. Take in the head, torso and four limbs. Feel your physicality – the sense of solidity in your body. This is the feeling of your tissue body. It's what we are very used to feeling. This is a residing feeling of tissues that provides us with a sense of being in the body.

Now contemplate the fact that tissues are collections of cells that are full of cytoplasm and bathed in extracellular fluid. Open up to the liquidity of your body. When it starts to reveal itself, it comes through as a melting of the physical body feelings. The body starts to become more amorphous and gel-like. The edges of the body start to become less distinct and the space around you becomes much more relevant. There is also a sense of expansion in the whole body as the fluid in you comes into your awareness.

This may need some practice. If the body is highly contracted, it can prevent this process. As you become more used to the feeling of fluid body, notice how much more energy emerges. The fluid body consists of many inter-relationships at the cellular level and brings you into a more conscious connection with its level of activity. In a way, you are in a more direct relationship with your physiology. The better you become at accessing your fluid body, the more you will move around in this state. There will be a residing feeling of oneness in your body, and bliss will be born as you deepen into it.

Meditation: fluid brain

At the centre of the fluid body is a fluid core. The body is designed such that the brain and spinal cord are floating in cerebrospinal fluid. This is unique in the body. The brain is highly fluid-like in its nature. Both on the inside and outside there is a volume of cerebrospinal fluid that bathes and buoys it up. The brain is literally afloat, so there's no surprise that this part of your body is able to easily drop into a fluid state. There is something particular about this fluid core that is unlike the fluid in the rest of the body: the remarkable phenomenon of water and electricity.

Somehow we have an ability to feel our central nervous system. Physically it has no receptors because it's where all receptors are received and processed. Your awareness seems to be able to go beyond that. You can feel your brain and spinal cord at the centre of your craniospinal axis. There's a definite feel to the brain and spinal cord in situ.

Be in relationship to your whole fluid body and the fluidity at your centre. Invite the deep fluid spaces of the brain to reveal themselves. They are called the ventricles of the brain and are large fluid spaces at its core. As they present to you, the feeling is of an expanding space deep at the centre of the head. Be open to a similar feeling emerging along the length of the spinal cord. There's an inner fluid space at the core of that, too. A particularly deep feeling of life and bliss comes to you as you become adept at this meditation, and that feeling becomes a permanent part of your system and daily experience.

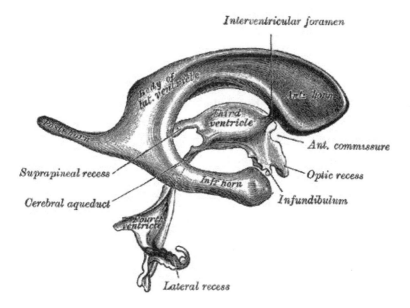

Figure 9.1 Ventricles

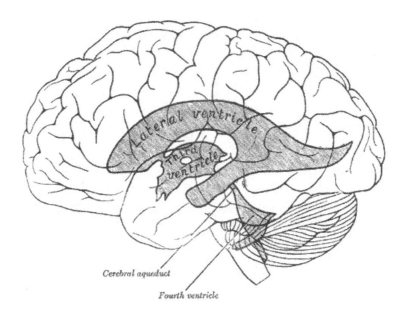

Figure 9.2 Ventricles in situ

An easy way into this meditation is to first let your body be still. Open up to the fluid sense of your head. If you stay with the feeling of your bones and invite them to melt, you will notice quite quickly how the cranium starts to feel amorphous. This leads to a sense of the whole head as being a fluid mass. Underneath the cranial bones is a highly fluid world. The brain is full of this fluid and is itself a soft structure. The very core of the brain will come into your awareness if you stay with this fluid-brain, fluid-cranium expression. When it does, there's a fullness and spaciousness to the ventricles that is unique in the body. The fullness is an aliveness and vitality in the fluids. This has the effect of charging your whole system up and settling the brain. Even though you are in relationship to the centre of your brain, you are in an expanded state. Notice the fluid–electrical mixture. Sit with this feeling for a few minutes.

Meditation: fluid heart

Sit still and let your chest relax and your breathing slow down. At the centre of your body and your chest is another powerful fluid organ: your heart. Its whole reason for being is to move a special fluid around the body. The heart is more like the brain than it initially seems from the outside. From the inside it is also electrical and fluid. Come into an awareness of your heart as a hollow structure that contains fluid plasma. These spaces are called ventricles and atria. The heart can melt into the fluid body, and as it does it reveals its inner fluid nature. A powerful health starts to show itself as you drop more and more deeply into the fluid heart. There's also a sense of expansion, not just in the whole body but beyond its boundaries, as well. This expansion makes *you* feel open and spacious. It also brings about a new relational field that can change your whole interaction with the world around you.

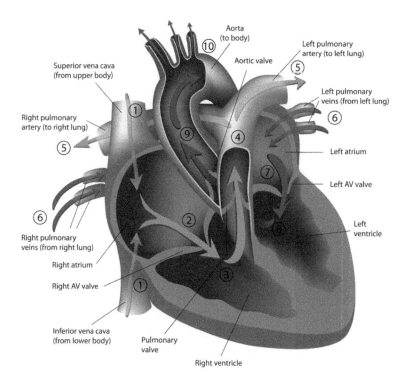

Figure 9.3 Heart and blood flow

CHAPTER 10

Being Centred

The body is whole. It's a living organism that is complete as a unit and all parts are equal in the wholeness; however, there is a persistent relationship defined by the body's history. The body has emerged from a craniospinal axis as a longitudinal phenomenon, and the rest of the body has developed from that. This gives the core of the body special significance. It's not only the home of the central nervous system but also the structural centre of the body. The vertebral column is the link for the rest of the body structures, so if you explore this axis at a number of levels, you will find a connection from the core to all parts of the body, and back. It's a reciprocal equilibrium. You could say everything 'hangs off the spine'. Everything relates to it, and in turn the spine reflects back to the rest of the body.

We started life as neural tubes and then built structure around that – a body – to protect it and move it around the planet. So the core of the body is strong and robust. There are a lot of bones and joints in there and most of the body's ligaments reside there. The body's structure is daring. It has produced a core that is both highly mobile and highly protected. That's quite a difficult architectural challenge. The vertebral column is a design wonder: 26 moving parts with over 100 joints. In fact, most of the body's joints are in this one structure. How does the column control and maintain biotensegrity? It uses lots of ligaments, swathes of tendon sheets and lots of membranes to hold it together with firmness and elasticity.

Being centred is being connected to our core, which is our axis from head to tail. The more present you are with this, the more intelligently the body moves and functions. So exploring the different elements of the axis will bring you into the nuances of movement and tissue cooperation. The body is at its best when there is a supple spine.

We all start life with the most fluid of bodies and spines, though quite quickly the body can grow and posture in a non-ideal way. We receive injuries and strains that leave their mark, and the body starts to compensate for deviations along the axis. The spine needs its curves for maximum efficiency. It needs a craniopelvic balance that allows weight distribution evenly throughout joints. Over time, the spine can lose its tensile energy and therefore a loss of motion, stability and balance. The body and mind are one. If the body is strained and lacking in mobility, the mind will follow suit.

If we can re-establish this core integrity and structural flexibility, our minds can be released. Static bodies and minds are uncreative. A body and core that is fluid-like is happy and inspired. The original design was created to generate maximum movement, so optimizing core strength and mobility is crucial to body mechanics.

EXPLORING YOUR VERTEBRAL COLUMN
Meditation: ligamentous midline

Sit comfortably and follow your breathing for a couple of minutes. Try to be natural in your breathing; don't try to change it. This meditation is a powerful way to come into awareness of your spinal joints and the whole of your vertebral column.

Using your breath, imagine that some of the air moves through a small portal at the back of your pharynx into the top vertebra of the atlas. Be gentle with the intention. This meditation is about bringing awareness through your breath into the big joints of the spine.

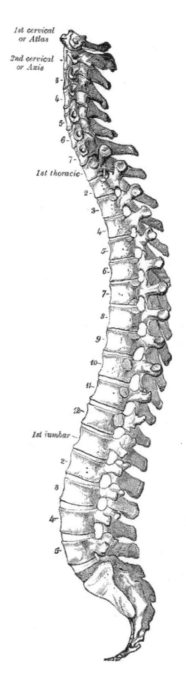

Figure 10.1 Vertebral column

Breathe into the atlas (first cervical vertebra) for a few breaths and then allow your breath to move down to the next vertebra, the axis. Again, use the breath to feel into the vertebral body and the disk joints between them. Following this sequence, work your way down all 7 cervical, 12 thoracic and 5 lumbar vertebrae over a 15-minute period. Once you reach the sacrum, breathe into the whole of it. You have now come into a deep awareness of your whole spinal column. Now try simply breathing into the whole spinal column for a few minutes. Once this is achieved, it's important to let go of the use of your breath. Imagine sealing up the portal at the back of your pharynx and taking your awareness away from your breathing. Now notice how the whole column is streaming with short and long ligaments that bind the vertebrae and disk joints into one continuous structure. Notice in particular the long ligaments at the front and back of the column that run its whole length. In reality, these ligaments are part of a whole ligamentous, tendinous, fascial continuum that binds the column into one supported connective tissue continuum.

Now relax and simply sit with a glowing spinal column.

THE CORE LINK

The dura mater is a deep fibrous skin of the brain. It has a balloon-like structure in the cranium and a long tube in the vertebral column. It attaches at the middle of the sacrum, but is free in the column, and again attaches in the foramen magnum of the cranium and in key places internally (Figure 10.2). This is a core membranous link from head to tail and is a highly defining structure. It's not something we notice consciously, but as you become more aware of it, you come into a sense of an important balanced tension at the very centre of your core. Allowing this membrane to come into its fullness and express its length and breadth without interruption can revolutionize the inner and outer structures, that is, the brain and spinal cord as well as the vertebral column and cranium. With practice of the meditation below, it's possible for structural issues and nervous irritations to clear up.

The falx and tentorium are strong organizing structures in the dura mater that have a particularly intimate connection to the vault bones in the cranium. Acknowledging bony membranous patterns can create healing effects on the functioning of all the meningeal layers and, thereby, also on the brain. An appreciation of these anatomical relationships is critical for good health.

The tentorium is a horizontal structure that attaches to the internal surface of the cranial vault and base bones. It's like a cranial diaphragm and its health and motion have wide-reaching effects. This membrane's balanced tension is important not just for structural integrity, but also for the easy flow of blood back from the cerebral hemispheres, as it contains a type of venous system for blood return. Any strain held within the tentorium will affect cranial bony dynamics as well as brain blood flow.

The tentorium and cranial bones are completely inter-related. Patterns in the tentorium will convey into the temporal bone, with which it commonly acts like a single unit of function, and this, in turn, will mirror into the pelvis.

Like the tentorium, the falx has a similar series of relationships with other cranial structures. The falx exerts a strong influence on the cranial bones and, through the dural tube, on the sacrum and pelvis. In many ways the dura mater is the infrastructure for the whole of the core, and re-establishing a sense of continuity and balanced tension along its length is valuable for whole-body awareness.

Meditation: core link

Using Figure 10.2, open up to your inner membranous cranium. The first thing you notice when you bring awareness to your cranium is its boniness. Underneath the bony layer is a much more elastic feeling that starts to shape your awareness into a balloon-like structure. This is the whole surround of the dura mater that creates the inner support for the brain. Follow the contours of it.

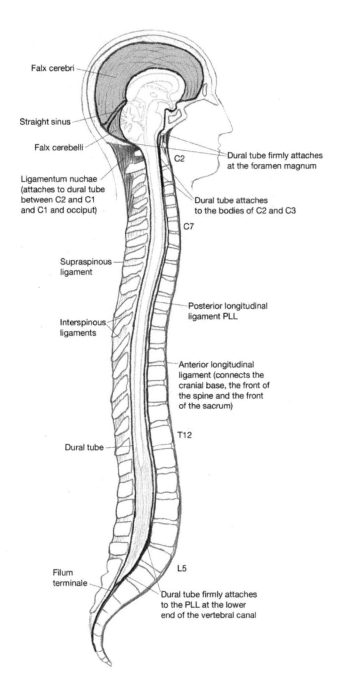

Falx cerebri

Straight sinus

Falx cerebelli

Ligamentum nuchae
(attaches to dural tube
between C2 and C1
and C1 and occiput)

Supraspinous
ligament

Interspinous
ligaments

Dural tube

Filum
terminale

C2

Dural tube firmly attaches
at the foramen magnum

Dural tube attaches
to the bodies of C2 and C3

C7

Posterior longitudinal
ligament PLL

Anterior longitudinal
ligament (connects the
cranial base, the front of
the spine and the front
of the sacrum)

T12

L5

Dural tube firmly attaches
to the PLL at the lower
end of the vertebral canal

Figure 10.2 Core link

There is a rich supply of sensory receptors that allow you to map the undulations of the sheet-like fabric. If you start at the bottom of the cranium and move your awareness upwards, you will follow the way the tentorium moves deep into the cranium around the ears, and how the falx moves deep between the cerebral hemispheres at the top of the cranium. Now stay with a whole sense of the cranial dura for a few minutes.

Try to follow the length of the dural tube as an extension of the cranial dura, from the foramen magnum at the bottom of the cranium all the way down through the vertebral column to the sacrum. Notice how free the dural tube feels in you.

Now you can be with a sense of the core link – the powerful membranous feeling from your sacrum to your crown. It has a natural continuity because it is one connective tissue system that contains and protects your central nervous system and gives your vertebral column inner elasticity. Notice any areas that are disrupting the continuity of tissues. Listen deeply to the story of your core link. Simply being with the sensations and feelings of this master membrane will generate an automatic release of repressed patterns and emotions, leading to a greater body awareness and sense of wholeness.

CRANIOPELVIC RESONANCE

How the cranium mirrors the pelvis is one of the basic relationships in the body. From the outside they look quite different, but a closer look reveals a deep mirroring of bones and membranes, cavities and joints, above and below. Key in this relationship are four joint complexes that dominate the balance of the whole craniospinal axis: the lumbosacral joint with the atlanto-occipital joint as well as the temporomandibular joint and the hip joints. If all four complexes can be in an easy joint dynamic, the knock-on effect through the whole core is substantial. The top and bottom of the spinal column powerfully influence each other. If one can find equilibrium, so can the other. Similarly, there is a mirrored relationship between your jaw and your hips.

THE TEMPOROMANDIBULAR JOINT AND THE HIP JOINTS

The jaw is an incredibly common place for holding tension. Many people grind or clench their teeth so much that they have to wear mouth guards and may have a history of dental problems. Commonly, these tensions are unconsciously held. The chewing muscles are amongst the most powerful muscles in the body, so the tension generated in this area can be intense and can affect many structures that are not just adjacent to the jaw. Long-term jaw tension has significance for the entire body. Try consciously sitting with your jaw held tightly for a minute. The experience quickly becomes an unpleasant feeling.

Why do we hold tension in our jaw? Mostly because of difficulty in communicating and expressing ourselves. The jaw can help us hold in emotions. All of this leads to tension in our musculoskeletal system and can impact down into the heart, gut, pelvic floor and hips.

MUSCLES OF THE JAW

The temporalis and masseter are familiar to most people and easily palpated on the external surfaces of the skull. On clenching the jaw, you can feel the fibres of the temporalis contracting on the side of the head superior and anterior to the ear. The masseter is easily felt passing from the zygomatic arch to the angle of the mandible.

Harder to feel and visualize are the very important pterygoid muscles, which are anchored on the pterygoid processes of the sphenoid. The medial pterygoid forms a sling with the masseter. The medial pterygoid, temporalis and masseter muscles all strongly close the jaw and are involved in chewing. Orienting to the sling of muscles is a very useful awareness practice.

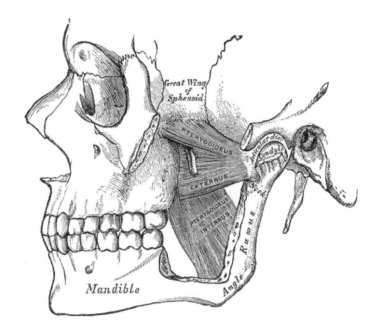

Figure 10.3 Pterygoids

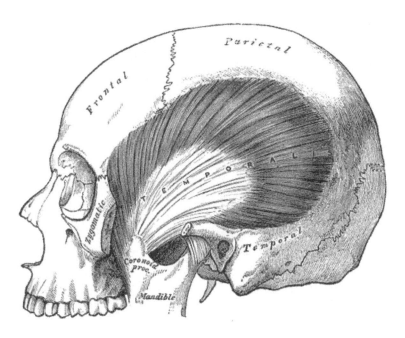

Figure 10.4 Temporalis

Meditation: letting go of your jaw

Huge tensions abound in your jaw, often hidden in the unconscious. Stress, pressure and anxiety can be held here more than in most places in the body. As the jaw muscles clench over long periods, the joints become compressed and dense. So the first thing to do is become aware of what's going on in your jaw and allow your body physiology to return to normal.

For this meditation, starting with your jaw, become aware of both sides of the lower jaw from the front at the chin to the back at ear. Consciously relax your chewing muscles. Let your tongue relax next and then the whole floor of your mouth. (Lots of the muscles here are linked to your chewing muscles.) Now let go of your upper jaw, which consists of your upper teeth and palate. Surprisingly strong compressions can be evident here. Let your lower jaw drop. The feeling is of hanging off the cranium. You might notice tensions in your throat as you do this, because the throat and jaw are deeply connected.

As you are consciously letting go of your jaw, notice how it affects your spinal column as well as your chest and pelvis. There is a powerful resonance into the hip joint area, which is deep in your groin, or the inguinal area at the top of your legs. As you continue letting go of your jaw, do the same at your groin. Let the muscles and ligaments soften. You will notice that helps the jaw to let go even more. Don't be surprised if there are surges of emotion as you do this.

For strong tensions repeat this exercise on a daily basis for a few days till the body finds a new balance.

SPINAL IMBALANCE

How common is it to have neck and lower back discomfort and pain? Just like the jaw and hip dynamic, there can be strong compensating tensions in both the neck and lumbar spine. Beneath all the muscular tension, however, is a powerful joint system that includes, in the case of the neck, the upper two vertebrae of the axis and atlas as well as the basal part of the occiput. This is like an upper triad of joint and ligament relationships. If there can be relief and balance in these top three structures, the whole spine will be modified by it.

Meditation: balancing the lumbosacral and atlanto-occiptal junctions

Spend time asking your structure at the top of the spine to let go of tension. You might notice some of the vertebrae moving around subtly to find a better position. Opening up to the whole spine, including the cranium and pelvis, will help this area reorganize even more. Remember that nothing in the body is independent. Every structure is a player in a whole-body orchestra. When the individual resonates with the whole structural body, that creates an intelligent, self-balancing body.

The second part of this meditation is to follow the same procedure for the other end of the vertebral column. Just like the top triad, there is a bottom triad of the bottom two lumbar vertebrae and the sacrum. Again, strong tension patterns can exist here in the muscles and tendons, but also the joints can be in poor alignment, leading to strain and compensations. Lots of the upper body weight passes through this joint complex, so its position is more critical than that of many other joint structures. Bringing your awareness to this area and discerning the tissues is a self-healing process. The more you are able to discriminate the different sensations in this area, the more the tissues become present to themselves and initiate automatic adjustments. The body can be blind to itself, but once there is clarity through presence, there is a natural reorganizing force that arises. It's this body intelligence that has been absent that makes the difference. Suddenly, the body is dynamic in its urge to adjust and reshape its form to an optimal biological balance. Repeating this meditation will familiarize you with the structures at the top and bottom of the spine and bring about a better core relationship and, in turn, a deep centring of both body and mind.

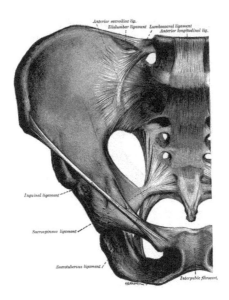

Figure 10.5 Lumbosacral junction

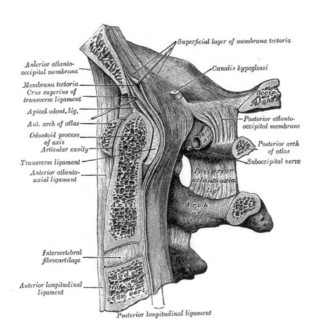

Figure 10.6 Atlanto-occipital junction

CHAPTER 11

Embryonic Mind

The human body is constructed in a wonderful way. The design of the body provides an explanation for some of the fundamental states of experience underlying our adult physiology and state of mind.

It's good to remember that we are basically a multicellular organism, a hive of 100 trillion cells, although we actually began life as a *single* cell. That first cell is the start of an explosion of cell division that carries on for the rest of our lives. All of our cells divide to produce new cells, and old cells die, so we are constantly replenishing cell numbers. What this says is that we are constantly changing. It's a dynamic change that happens in relation to a template, but nevertheless we literally are not the same person we were. Why is it, then, that we feel permanent and solid when, in fact, we are in a constant state of flux?

Different cells live for different lengths of time. The cells that tend to be replaced most quickly are epithelial cells. These cells line all the surfaces of the body: skin, gut, lungs and airways. You can see how these cells would need replenishing. We have lots of these cells and, in fact, they have the highest turnover. All other cells have a typical lifetime, for example, red blood cells live 4 months before they wear out and liver cells up to a year. Cells lining the gut have the shortest lifetime, only 5 days. The average lifespan of most other cells is around 7–10 years. The only exception are the neurons of the central nervous system and the heart muscle cells. There's a debate about how much these cells can renew themselves, as recently stem cells have been discovered in both the brain and heart. We have various lifespans within us, ranging from hours to days to years to a whole lifetime. Our bodies are a mix of permanence and impermanence, and the most permanent places are the heart and brain.

The brain and heart developed from simple tubes into mature structures. The laying down of neurons and cardiac cells significantly slows down around the age of 2 years and stops for the brain around the age of 7 years, after which you have your allotted number of brain cells for the rest of your life. If cells carry our consciousness, then our sense of permanence may well emanate from these cells and our sense of impermanence from cells that are constantly dividing and replenishing themselves.

There's something significant about neurons, as they are the first cells to form a significant structure, the neural tube The neural tube emerges from the embryonic disk and from the embryonic spaces. It becomes the very centre of the body (more on this below).

The heart is similar in its beginnings in that it starts as a simple tube that loops and folds and then builds a complex muscular and nervous system around it that becomes the centre of a whole circulatory system. The heart and its beat have been with us for a long time, created by the cardiac cells that we generated in utero.

FLUID CORE

The embryonic origin of the neural tube is fascinating. The images in Figure 11.1 show how the body generates tissues and structures around the simple tube as the primary axis of the body. The important thing to understand is that the tube is formed from the back space of the developing embryo.

By the end of its first week of life, the fertilized ovum goes through a series of powerful shifts to produce an egg-like structure with a front and back compartment around a disk. The disk is important as it forms an interface between the two compartments that will become the palette for the generation of the first body structures, starting with the neural tube. The other important concept is that this rudimentary form of the early embryo is essentially generating a front and back space first, before the body emerges at the meeting of the two.

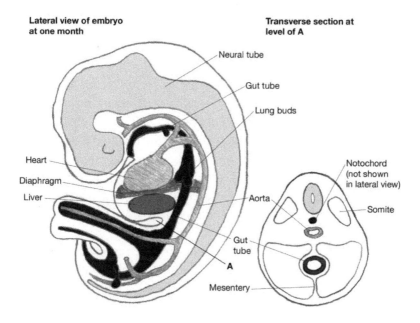

Figure 11.1 Embryonic midline

The neural tube is the first structure to emerge that persists into the adult form. It's formed by the welling up of the ectoderm layer to form a tube out of the fluid from the back cavity, called the amniotic cavity. The body then starts to form itself around these simple, tube-like concentric rings, which are like the rings of a tree. As the growth occurs outwards, the body layers up and generates its membranes, bones and joints on top of the original tube. It also creates cavities, organs, bony and muscle surrounds, and then the limbs. The point is that all of the body has grown out from this first structure, a hollow tube. The amazing thing is that the tube still exists within us. It has never changed since day 23 after conception when it came into formation. At the very centre of our body is the axis, and the very centre of that is our central nervous system, and the very centre of that is our fluid tube. Anatomists call this the ventricles and central canal.

There are a number of important conclusions from all of this. Number one is that we are fluid at our core and always have been fluid. This fluid space is the original growth space of the body. If we can connect with it, there is a deep acknowledgement of the origins of our body. Something quite profound can be experienced in terms of health and balance.

The second thing is that the brain has a centre that is a fluid space where there is no brain tissue, just empty space that is fluid-filled. The fluid in the adult is cerebrospinal fluid and in the embryo it is amniotic fluid. The fluid spaces buoy the brain up and make it lighter and more cushioned, but there's something else significant about them: there's a non-structural core at the centre of the most complex part of our body. The hugely complex brain has emerged out of nothing and still needs a relationship to non-form to maintain its balance. It needs the simplicity of nothing at its centre to run well.

The third thing is that the neural tube is generated from the back space of the body that becomes the whole fluid surround. Figure 11.2 shows how the amniotic space of the foetus has an intrinsic relationship to the centre of our brain and spinal cord, as does the skin and the central nervous system. What does this mean in our lives? It means that our environment is in a deep relationship to our core.

The fourth thing is that there is an embryonic mind within us. It's a fluid mind that is not based on neurons or glial cells but rather water and space. When you connect to this space, the mind goes through the most remarkable shifts.

Meditation: fluid origin

Bring your awareness to your whole body and its volume. Notice the motion of the body. Now come into felt sense of your axis. At the core of this is a fluid centre line. Invite this aspect of your body into your awareness. Stay with it for a couple of minutes. Now open up to the immediate space around you. Open out to it with your whole body as if it's a part of you. Imagine that the space around you is fluid-like. Notice the resonance between the fluid surround and your fluid centre. Notice, too, how it is to be in awareness of both centre and periphery, and what that does to your mind and body.

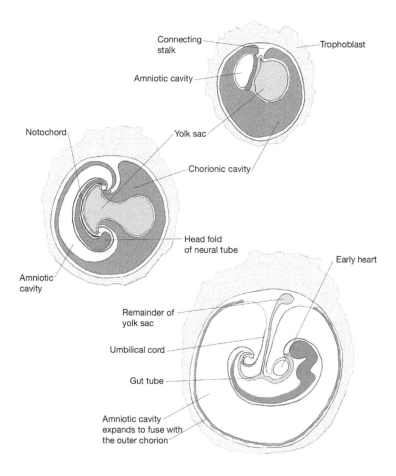

Figure 11.2 Morphology of fluid spaces

PRIMAL SPACES

It's fascinating that the body structures take a while to form in the early days of the embryo. Nothing we call our body shows up for the first 2 weeks after conception. This period of life is quite mysterious and reveals some remarkable insights into the forces that generate form. Basically, the first week consists of a proliferation of cells within a confined space to produce a cluster of 32 cells, which reach a critical mass at day 4. Lots of the cells at the centre of the cluster die through lack of nutrients and collapse, releasing their cell fluid into the core of the cluster. This death of cells so soon after the creation of cells gives rise to a fluid-filled cyst, which has an internal fluid space and a membrane. It is arguably our first body.

Once the blastocyst is embedded in the uterine wall, it starts to create two more fluid spaces. These are primal spaces that are essentially the space in front and at the back of the body, plus an even bigger surround out from those two spaces. The best way to see it is in Figure 11.3. At this point there is still nothing that will become the body. These are the fluid spaces that create the right environment for emergence of a neural tube along the centre of the embryonic disk. So you could say the fluid spaces are intelligent spaces that bring about the generation of the neural tube. Below is a mighty meditation based on this, which will bring you into contact with your original health and open up a living connection to the space around the body.

Meditation: primal spaces

Bring your awareness to the front of your body, the whole front palette from forehead to chest to front of legs and feet. Now open up to the space in front of you. Part of your receptivity is able to feel the space, so suspend any scepticism you may have and simply be open to it. Is there a sense of volume that comes to you? Are there sensations that arise? Now do exactly the same with the space behind you. Does it feel different from the front? Stay with it for a minute or two and then be interested in the coronal plane of your body. If you touch the sides of your head and move your hands up and out to the sides, it would be along what was the meeting place of these two spaces and the location of the embryonic disk. Allow the front and back spaces to come into contact with each other around this plane. What do you notice? Now open up to an even bigger space out from the front and back spaces and containing them both. How big is that and what does it feel like? Stay with it for a minute or two. These are the primal spaces of the body that give rise to midline structures that form the core of the body.

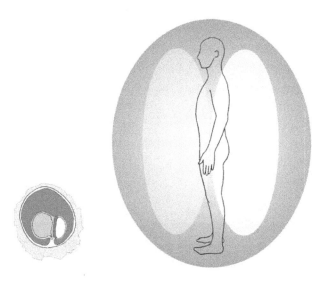

Figure 11.3 Primal spaces

FIRST CELL

As mentioned previously, we all started life as a single cell. What the first cell generates is the biggest cell we ever have – a hundred times bigger than our regular cells. That cell is also totipotent, meaning that it can become any cell. It's basically the blueprint for all cells, and all cells in our body are related to it. Every time there's a cell division, there's a connection made to the first cell. The body generates millions of new cells per second and the whole expression of the first cell is constantly taking place. Our body energy at the cellular level is like a nuclear power station, and the creative energy of our first cell is still available. Its blueprint is still running in the body, so if we can tap into that level of health within us, the body as a physiological unit can be transformed.

Meditation: zygote

Bring your awareness to your skin. This is your body membrane, which mimics the membrane of our smallest unit – the cell. The cell has a fluid interior with organelles and a nucleus, plus an infrastructure called the cytoskeleton. This is essentially the same as the body. We have organelles, we have a skeleton and connective tissues, and we have a centre: the brain and spinal cord. Open up to your body as a reflection of its cells so that you drop into a direct relationship with your body at a cellular level. Try not to intellectualize; instead, simply notice what happens when you resonate with your cells. Stay with it for a few minutes and then sit with your body as one giant cell. Your zygote. Be interested in the internal and external relationships across your skin as the cell membrane, and most importantly, feel the energy that is generated. There is an energy here that was generated at conception.

Figure 11.4 Zygote

CHAPTER 12

Internal and External Circulation

After breathing, the biggest movement in your body is the flow of the cardiovascular system. There are 9–12 pints of blood flowing like a torrent around your body. We are unconscious to its movements, but dropping into a felt sense awareness of it brings a richness of sensations.

There are many different speeds at which blood flows, and feeling into the detail of this reveals a body that is organized primarily around capillary beds. These are the very fine single-cell-thick vessels that populate every inch of our body. Indeed, every structure within us is organized around these fine vessels. When we think about blood and circulation, we think heart and major blood vessels, but those structures are a small part of the circulatory system, which is actually predominantly about capillaries.

Capillaries are the part of the system that comes into contact with the cells of the body. They bring blood to the space between cells known as the interstitial space. The circulatory system has different speeds: arterial, venous, capillary and lymphatic. The different speeds are all unique and blood moves fast in certain places, slower in others and languishes in still other places. The other thing about blood is its health. It's the fluid of life, and just forming a felt sense awareness of it brings out a feeling of bliss and energy.

RED BLOOD CELLS

The most prolific cell in your body is the red blood cell (RBC), which accounts for 25% of all cells. These cells are unique in their shape. We've all seen how they are disk-like with a squeezed centre. All cells are unique and the RBC is unique in that it is highly mobile. It's on the move around your body from the lungs to the heart to the intercellular space. Most cells in the body are fixed. Only RBCs and some white blood cells (WBCs) have the ability to move freely.

In humans, mature RBCs are flexible and oval bi-concave disks. They lack a cell nucleus and therefore contain neither deoxyribonucleic acid (DNA) nor most organelles, in order to accommodate maximum space for haemoglobin. Approximately 2.4 million new RBCs are produced per second! The cells develop in the bone marrow and circulate for about 100–120 days in the body before their components are recycled by macrophages. Each circulation takes about 20 seconds. So a quarter of your body's cells are on the move all the time. Next time you feel stuck, just think of your RBCs and you will feel mobilized. We are not by nature fixed. We are both fixed and free in our cell types.

Red blood cells are a total phenomenon. They are strong and flexible, and they squeeze in and out of capillaries. Each RBC has over a trillion interactions with other cells in its lifetime. No wonder it wears out and needs breaking down. Your spleen has WBCs that remove 100 billion RBCs from your blood every day, so that means your bone marrow needs to produce 100 billion RBCs per day to replace them. No wonder your red bone marrow is one of the most active places in your body – a factory spewing out 2.4 million RBCs per second. That level of furious activity is very difficult to visualize. The whole of your living skeleton is engaged in this effort day and night. So if you ever feel tired, just drop into conscious relationship with the power of your marrow and you will feel revitalized. These cells are remarkable in that they spin and create a centrifugal force that gives energy to your blood. This energy enables the blood to circulate, because the heart alone is not enough to move such a large volume of fluid. Blood is helped by the internal motility of the RBCs and the internal shape of the arteries and veins to help the blood spiral.

Meditation: red blood cells

Spend time looking at the image of a RBC. This is a unique shape in your body and merely looking at it will start a connection to your RBC population. (If you were to look at an image of a liver cell, you would get a different feeling.) There are sensations generated from RBCs that create a unique felt sense signature. Use the image as a meditation object. Stare at it for a couple of minutes and then close your eyes and be with your whole-body awareness. Repeat this several times so that you sink more deeply into the relationship.

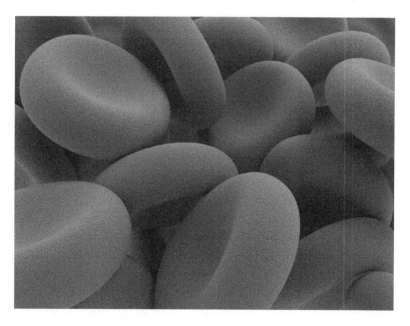

Figure 12.1 Red blood cells

HEART OF BONES

The vertebral bodies, pelvis, flat bones of the ribcage and cranium as well as the proximal ends of the long bones of the limbs contain red bone marrow. This is where RBCs, WBCs and platelets are formed. The distal bones of the limbs and the central portion of the femur and humerus also contain yellow marrow, which is a fat deposit for energy and insulation. Red bone marrow is one of the most potent and active places in the body, and this generates a lot of heat and energy. Bones are humming with activity and are well supplied with blood. Red marrow contains pluripotent, hematopoietic stem cells. These stem cells can become RBCs, WBCs (leukocytes) or platelets. All these different cells are then carried throughout the body via the circulatory system. The WBCs are the foundation of the immune system, so contact into the marrow is a direct connection into the immune system. It is like connecting into a slow-burning power.

Meditation: power of the marrow

Come into awareness of the proximal long bones of one arm and one leg. Proximal is the part nearest the torso. The intention here is to connect with the length and density of the humerus and femur. Acknowledge the array of tissues and fluids in the bones.

Open up to the long-bone structure and be curious about the interior of the long bone. Feel the activity of the bone marrow.

Now open up to a feeling of potency at the centre of the bones. There is a constant activity in the marrow that can't be missed. As the marrow comes more fully into your consciousness, open up to the blood capillaries and the circulatory flow that is part of the phenomenon of the marrow.

Widen your awareness to include the whole circulatory system. Opening up to the whole circulatory system will open up a perceptual window to the immune system. Finally, feel what happens when you open up to the marrow of the whole body. You are in contact with the whole skeletal system, and at the core of that is the body's marrow.

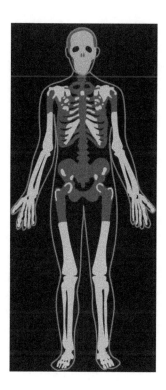

Figure 12.2 Marrow

BLOOD FLOW

The big movements in the body come from breathing and circulation. If your heart and lungs stopped and your blood stopped moving, existence would be a much quieter affair. In deep meditation both of these slow down and the body accesses another level of health.

It's necessary that much of the body's internal movements be filtered out of our everyday consciousness. But when you do start to attune to the movement of blood, there is a unique form of sensation and power that can be highly inspiring and often ecstatic.

Below are a few experiential exercises that will bring you into relationship with your circulatory system. The easiest way to find your blood is to listen to your heart. The heart quickly reveals what it is pumping. There's a deepening into the internal chambers of the heart. The heart is hollow and fluid-filled, and once you acknowledge the nervous energy and muscular contraction of the heart, you will come into relationship with its fluids. How can you miss it? The heart pumps over 40 gallons a day. As soon as you gain a sense of the inner spaces of the heart and the fluid movements, you will sense the RBCs, as they constitute 40–45% of the blood's volume.

Meditation: circulatory system

A wonderful journey begins where you can follow blood in its different forms, through the arterial system to the cells – the interstitial or intercellular space – then into the venous system to return back to the heart. There is a big difference between arterial and venous flow, like two different gears in your body. The arterial flow is fast and highly charged, whereas the venous flow is much slower, as the blood has denatured; so has the plasma, as now there is carboxylic acid in it. Being in felt sense awareness of these blood flows amplifies the effect in your body, and you will notice that a deep rhythm is set for the whole body system. Let's also explore the pivot for both systems in the heart and diaphragm. The diaphragm is the pump for the venous return. Shallow movement of the diaphragm results in oedema, which impacts hugely on our sense of energy and vitality. So sit comfortably and let your breathing relax. If you bring your awareness to your chest you will be able to tune into the beat of your heart. Open up to the blood flow moving through the heart and follow the most powerful surge of blood into the aorta, which curls over the heart and round the back of it before moving down the length of the body. Feel the power and speed of the blood. You can follow the blood as it moves out from the heart in all directions via the major arteries.

Let's be interested in the meeting of the arterial and venous blood flows in the biggest part of the circulatory system, the capillary beds. These beds are ultra-fine networks of vessels that cover the whole body (i.e. all cells). The large vasculature only accounts for the gross parts of the system, but the finer capillaries account for a much bigger network. The capillary beds are hugely potent places of health as one system shifts into another – a real meeting of complementary energies and different aspects of us. Now shift your awareness to the movement of blood returning to the heart from your extremities. This will bring you into the venous system. Notice how different the tone of this is from the arterial flow. Much slower. Notice, too, the effect it has on your body. It's calming.

Now let's follow the third part of the circulatory system, the movement of lymph. This is the process of cleaning the interstitial fluids through a slow osmosis into very fine lymphatic vessels located everywhere in the body. There are no RBCs here; instead, there is a very slow movement of plasma. The lymphatic system does not have a pumping mechanism to move lymph fluid around the body. The system relies on the contraction of muscles and movement of the body to move the fluid along fine capillary-like vessels to clusters of nodes. This part of the circulatory system is one of the major aspects of the immune system. White blood cells inhabit the nodes and act to stop bacteria from invading your body and increasing bacterial populations. Like following the venous return, you are interested in a much slower movement that is more like a trickling of fluid from the periphery to the core and then to the heart. It's a fine, subtle movement right in the background of your system. Notice how it moves through key junctions like lock gates at the meeting of the limbs with the torso and around the neck and mouth and all around the gut. These are called lymph nodes and slow the movement of the lymph down to clean and detoxify it. Just listening to the flow and relaxing in these key areas can produce better flow. The most remarkable thing about tuning into your lymph is that it slows everything down and brings this stillness to the mind and body. It's good to know something in your body is moving so slowly.

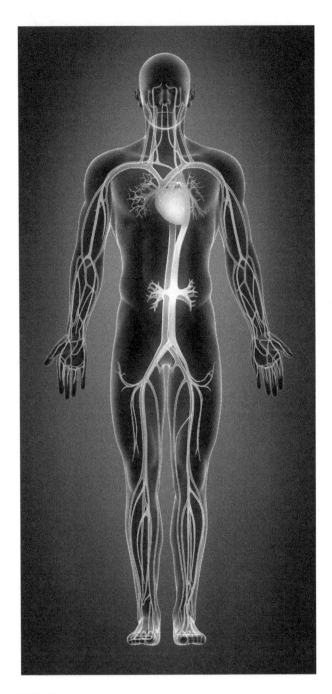

Figure 12.3 Circulatory system

UMBILICAL CIRCULATION

There are three major life events before we are born. The first event occurs at day 23 after conception and is the biggest movement we ever make. It's the changing of the embryo into a C-shaped entity. The next event is the heart starting to beat. The third event is the umbilicus linking up to the maternal blood supply. This series of events occurs in phases over several weeks and finally gets established at week 8. Up to this point the embryo amazingly has been living off its own resources, generating millions of cells and building form from its own energy supply (at least that's how it seems!). The embryo creates its yolk and then lives off it for several weeks until it finds a constant supply of nutrition through the placenta. It's as if something is being created out of nothing.

The umbilicus is a remarkable system that sends blood from the heart via the pelvis and umbilicus out to the mother's placenta. The embryo has created everything right up to the placental capillaries. We spend a long time in utero floating in a fluid bag, creating our form and being fed glucose and oxygen to run this process. It is noteworthy that we weren't so internalized then. Our blood was leaving our bodies out into the fluid space in which we lived to return recharged. What an amazing relationship to have had, and the remarkable thing is that it was freely given. In other words, we were growing without strife and nature was nurturing us.

Even though we have grown up into independent beings, there is still something of this early development within us. It's held in a much subtler form: we no longer have umbilical cords and amniotic spaces, but we do have an environment with which we are deeply enmeshed, and reconnecting with the umbilical system is a way to come into this natural environmental connection. The body tissues still remember the significance of the umbilicus, and as you will see from the meditation below, there is an essential connection between your heart and blood as well as a natural buoyant energy within your system that often can be disrupted by experiences at birth.

UMBILICAL EFFECTS

There's a common event at birth that involves immediate clamping and cutting of the cord. The baby's body makes a huge shift in its internal mechanisms that switch on the pulmonary circuit and switch off the umbilical network. This takes place rapidly as the head is crowning and the baby is being born into the world of air. It must be quite a shock transitioning from fluid to air. The baby's physiology needs time to let the circulatory system settle, so if this process is rushed, there can be any number of umbilical traumatic effects: implosion or shock in the gut and enteric nervous system as well as in the mesentery and lumbar arch. This shock effect can also continue up the umbilical vein into the liver and heart, or down the artery into the inguinal area and pelvic floor. Such an event can disturb the baby and create issues around feeding and digestion, as well as difficult emotional reactions, which, if not resolved, can go on into adult life. Often these feelings can generate a sense of being cut off and disconnected from the environment – that is, dissociated. Repeating the exercise below can result in a deep healing of the early shock and trauma that is behind many symptom pictures.

Meditation: umbilical stream

Using Figure 12.4, start this meditation with a connection to your heart. Simply wait and truly feel the beat of your heart. The whole body is subtly being moved by this beat. Next, follow the blood out into the aortic arch and then down the aorta. This is the strongest movement of your blood and therefore the easiest to feel. Follow the artery to where it bifurcates at the pelvis. The umbilical veins have become the median ligaments that start from your groin and move up to the umbilicus itself. Imagine these veins still exist and blood is flowing along them. Now open up to a subtle streaming out from your umbilicus into the space around you. Imagine that you are back in the womb and there's a fluid and membranous cavity around you. Follow the movement of blood out to the placenta. Notice how easy this feels and/or how readily sensations come to you. The veins spiral out. Then do the opposite: follow the movement of blood back to the umbilicus from the placenta via the umbilical artery.

Again, notice how this feels. When it comes into the umbilicus, the artery turns 90 degrees and moves upwards through what is now the round ligament and the falciform ligaments of the liver, and then it joins the vena cava back to the heart.

Stay with the umbilical circuit for a few minutes. Let your body float in the space around you and surrender to the ebb and flow of the blood supply. How do you feel emotionally? What are the feelings in other parts of your body?

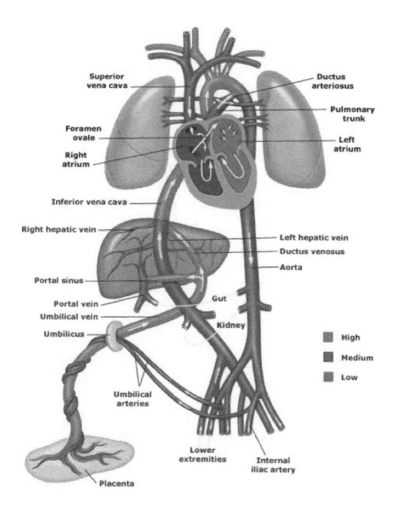

Figure 12.4 Umbilical stream

CHAPTER 13

Inner Cell

Cells are not insentient. The body is, after all, made up of cells, and they create the most remarkable function and structure. The body is incredibly intelligent; therefore, its smallest unit, the cell, must be. The cell has gone from being a blob of cytoplasm with a dark stain at the centre to a highly complex interactive organism. Over the past 40 years science has revealed the deep complexity of the cell. Each cell is like a creature that feels and reacts to its environment in a sensitive and intelligent way. Cell membranes are particularly smart. Not only is it the skin of the cell, but also it has thousands of delicate feelers coming off it, called receptors, that are stimulated by substances in the fluid environment around the cell.

This chapter opens us up to who we are at a micro level – a hive of cells that has derived incredible abilities to work together to form all of the miraculous parts of the body. Add to this the ability to stay in intense relationship with each other so that the whole community of cells has an intelligence in itself that is greater than that of any particular group of cells. So getting to know the cell has got to be one of the best things we can do, because it means getting in touch with our basic unit. The whole of life starts from one cell, and even though the cell has become a city of cells, its nature is still 'cellular'. So let's spend time finding our inner cell.

The level of activity in the cell is beyond comprehension. Each cell could be thought of as a metropolis. It has become clear that the cell is much more structured than originally thought. The structures themselves are all quite unique and have specific functions so that they are now called organelles, as if they are organs within the body of the cell. The cell is no different from the structural body. We have a skin and we have a connective tissue mainframe, and held in this framework are the organs.

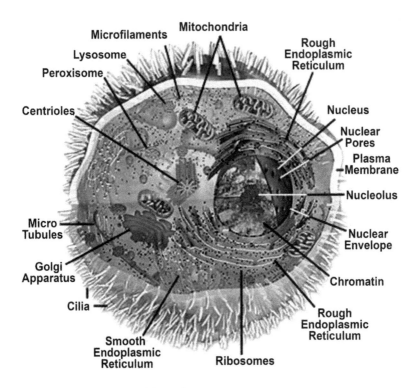

Figure 13.1 Anatomy of the cell

ASPECTS OF THE CELL

Let's look at some of the major aspects of the cell (Figure 13.1). The biggest part is the cytoplasm. There's something surprising about cytoplasm: It's alive. It's not just water, it's protoplasmic, meaning 'first thing formed'. There's a mix of electrolytes and ions, amino acids, monosaccharides and water, and macromolecules such as nucleic acids, proteins, lipids and polysaccharides. So it's actually a highly complex fluid that can change its state from solid to gel and back again. Single-cell creatures, for example, an amoeba, use this characteristic to move themselves. The cytoplasm also exhibits protoplasmic streaming, which is a poorly understood phenomenon. It is like an internal circulation of the fluid volume within the cell to distribute nutrients. In any case, these properties exhibit how alive cytoplasm is.

Next, let's look at the cell membrane, which is a sandwich-like structure with lipid molecules surrounding a cholesterol centre. The cholesterol makes the membrane impermeable to water, so water solution on the inside cannot mix with water solution on the outside without the membrane allowing this through the conscious opening of pores. It's a clever and simple system that works through the vast array of receptors on the membrane surface.

Our cells are hairy. A typical neuron cell, for example, may contain millions of receptors on its surface. These receptors are generally long-chain glyco- or lipoproteins. Each cell has hundreds of different kinds of receptors waving around like a sea anemone's tentacles. Most receptors are transmembranous, meaning that they cross the membrane barrier and conduct a signal into the interior of the cell. So the cell membrane is all about communication and information streaming from the outside to the inside of the cell. Meditating on your cell membranes will increase your membrane function and receptor ability to bind with all the different hormones and secretions in the body. Receptors can be bent out of shape by trauma and pathology. Being skilled at finding this felt sense in your system can bring about changes at a fundamental level. The cell membrane has a tensegrity of its own that creates a wave-like movement across the whole surface area of the membrane. This membrane movement is a dynamic part of the cell's natural movement called motility. It's worth remembering that all your cells are descended from a single cell that had an ability to survive and move independently.

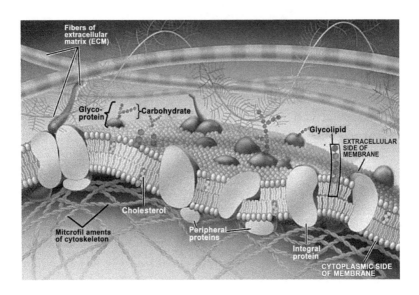

Figure 13.2 Cell membrane

The next thing to explore is the nucleus. The nucleus is a bank of DNA that is constantly being stimulated to reveal genetic codes for the cell making all the different substances necessary for the running of the body. So DNA is unwinding its triple helix to show codes for making mucus, collagen, keratin, hormones, etc. The body manufactures a lot of substances and each cell is part of that process. Your cell nucleus, therefore, is highly active. Your DNA is not just sitting there!

Here are some amazing facts about DNA:

- It is found inside every cell in our body (apart from RBCs).

- Each cell contains roughly 2 metres of DNA. (Humans have roughly 100 trillion cells.)

- If you unravelled all of your DNA from all of your cells and laid out the DNA end to end, the strand would stretch from the Earth to the Sun hundreds of times. (The Sun is approximately 98 million miles away from Earth.)

- You could fit 25,000 strands of DNA side by side in the width of a single adult hair.

Cells, and therefore the body, are composed of five substances: salt water, protein, carbohydrate, fat and nucleic acid. As you can see from the above facts, we have a lot of nucleic acid in us. So coming into awareness of your DNA means coming into relationship with a substance in your body that is completely different from everything else, and the felt sense awareness therefore feels unique.

Figure 13.3 DNA

MITOCHONDRIA

Mitochondria are your inner cell batteries. The lung/heart phenomenon is the outer respiration for delivering oxygen and glucose to every cell in the body, and the mitochondria are the site for true respiration, which is the combining of oxygen and glucose. The mitochondria are highly potent places that generate high-energy molecules called adenosine triphosphate (ATP). This is the energy molecule of your body (Figure 13.4). The more ATP the merrier!

Try staring at the image of the molecule while you come into your felt sense awareness. The body knows this molecule so well that just referencing it through an image is enough to highlight it in your biochemistry. There's a lot of effort going on in the body – heart pumping, blood circulating, lungs breathing, manufacture of RBCs, digestion of food, etc. – that is all done to produce this one molecule. The energy generated from oxygen and glucose combining together changes the adenosine diphospate molecule to ATP, which is a higher-energy molecule. This is the molecule that drives every molecular reaction in your body. It's the energy 'currency' of the body.

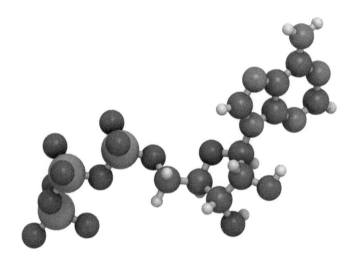

Figure 13.4 ATP

CYTOSKELETON

The inside is like the outside. The cell is like the body. The body is modelled on the cell. The amazing connective tissue system of the body is reflective of the cell's connective tissue system. It's called the cytoskeleton, and instead of collagen it is actin, another kind of protein, which shapes itself into microfilaments and tubules to create an inner framework that gives the cell shape and internal order. All the organelles of the cell attach to it, just like the organs of the body. Cells in turn hang onto the connective tissue system of the body, as everything seems to need a framework.

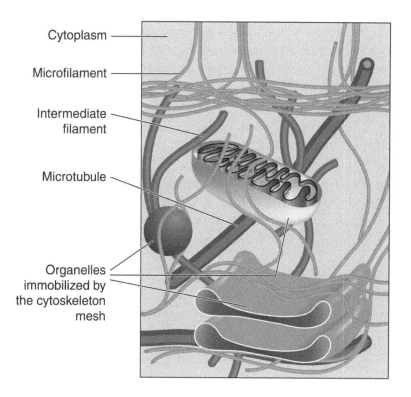

Cytoplasm

Microfilament

Intermediate filament

Microtubule

Organelles immobilized by the cytoskeleton mesh

Figure 13.5 Cytoskeleton

CELL/BODY CONTINUUM

Cells and their internal components are not separate or out of relationship with the rest of the body. That's the important thing to understand: there is a continuum between cells and the structural world we experience – arms and legs, eyes and mouth, heart and stomach. We are deeply aware of this level of the body. Can we be aware of cells and molecules? The answer is that we already are experiencing these things. Your arm is made up of muscles, bones and ligaments, all of which are made up of cells. Our physical receptors give our brains information down to the cellular level. Muscle spindle fibres, to name just one receptor, measure the contractility of muscle fibres, which are cells. If we become sensitive to our body, we can shift a whole gear from gross perception to a nuanced perception that includes cells. That actually brings us into connection with a whole other layer of energy within us. The problem with health is that we often don't experience the depths of it, and we are therefore not in relationship with the huge reservoir of energy within us.

Meditation: hierarchy of levels

Let's go through a process of deepening from the gross to the fine. Close your eyes and notice the whole body. Be with a sense of your whole system. This is the integrated you. Now shift your perception to a sense of individual systems within the whole such as the nervous system or the gastrointestinal tract. Stay with this state of perception for a while.

Now shift your perception to the world of individual organs and structures. Notice the kidney or individual bones. What is the quality of this? Now shift to the tissue field. Notice the different kinds of tissues in the body and how they blend together. Be interested in which tissues show themselves to you. Again, stay with this for a short while.

Shift again to a sense of the cellular level of the body. Try visualizing the cell as a way to connect with this level of organization. See if you can come into a sense of the cell through the interstitial space, that is, through the extracellular fluid. This should open up a relationship with the intracellular fluid and the cell membrane. Stay with this for a few minutes.

Shift again to the molecular world within you. This is the world of chemical activity and metabolic fields. The cell is a factory of intense chemical activity. See if you can relate to this. What comes to you? Shift again to the smallest unit within you, the atom and the subatomic world. Do you have a sense of the energy held within the smallest unit of the body and the universe? Has the energy feeling in your body changed? Now wonder why we ever get tired.

CELL CONSCIOUSNESS

So, as we now know, we are a collection of cells. Is it possible that our consciousness resides within our cells? If so, then the cell represents a major aspect of our consciousness and the kind of cells we have are aspects of that, too. So getting to know them is the same as getting to know all the parts of your consciousness. Here's a definition of the word 'consciousness': awareness of one's own existence, sensations, thoughts, surroundings, etc. That's a wonderful definition, particularly the etcetera – it seems to mean everything. So if consciousness is awareness of existence and a powerful part of awareness is felt sense awareness, if you increase your felt sense awareness, you increase your existence. Becoming more present to your body constitutes greater consciousness. If you are body aware, you are smart and healthy. People who struggle around this 'exist' less. When there is dissociation, there is a movement away from feeling the body and being with your cells. Dysfunction comes about through a lack of relationship to our cells.

MEDITATIONS TO ENHANCE YOUR RELATIONSHIP TO YOUR CELLS
Meditation: resonance of cell membrane and body membrane

Bring your awareness to the outline of your body. Open up to the feeling of your skin and track it in its entirety. The skin is your outer membrane and boundary with the world around you. Its nature is a whole-body wrap. Start with the skin of your hands and connect with the skin of your arms and upper body, and let the entirety of the skin come to you. This can be quick, as the skin is a massive connective tissue that spreads out like a matrix in all directions. The fullness of the skin feels like an elastic bag containing all the structures of the body; its elasticity enables movement. Marvel at your skin and its function. Remember that the body is modelled on the cell and is in so many ways like a cell. The cell has a cytoplasm, organelles and a cytoskeleton. The body has organs and a skeleton, too, and is mostly fluid. Open up to the interior of the body as a fluid space. The body can quickly show a fluid membranous state because that is its nature. At the same time, imagine that the space immediately around you is a fluid space. The body was formed in a fluid membranous space for 9 months and the skin matured in this environment. As you start to imagine this fluid space around you, open up to your cells. This is a mirrored relationship. All cells are in a fluid space called the interstitial space. Like the skin of the body, the cell membrane is the interface between two sets of fluids. Be open to the tensile quality of the cell membrane. It's a physical force within you that aggregates into a membranous whole-body feeling.

Meditation: cytoplasm

Drop into awareness of your whole body. Be interested in how much of your body feels fluid-like. Open up to the amount of fluid residing in your body (nearly 9 gallons). This is your fluid body. It's like the cell in that it's a reflection of your smallest unit. The body fluids are based on cytoplasm, which is the first fluid of our existence. When we form as a first cell, our parents' cytoplasm has helped populate our first cell with this fluid. Sink into the feeling of your fluid body. The largest fluid expression is the intracellular fluid volume, which is cytoplasm. Simply sit in your cytoplasm. Let the energy and intelligence of this fluid space refresh your system.

Meditation: chromosome

Follow the above meditation. Once you've been in the cytoplasmic state for a while, use Figure 13.3 to connect with your DNA. This molecule is unique in our bodies, and the long, spiral double-helix chain has a very particular resonance to it. Feel your DNA.

CHAPTER 14

Hormonal Space

The basis of the body and health is the balance of the neuroendocrine immune (NEI) system. Health can be thought of as the music played by the coordinated NEI orchestra. In the body, however, there is no real conductor, just the system moving together as a sentient whole.

Increasingly, biological science shows that the responses of the central nervous system, endocrine system and immune system cannot be separated. Any discussion of the interaction of these systems necessitates understanding the experience of emotion and stress. The inner state that is emotion is largely unconscious and is the result of the network of interactions within the NEI system.

Glands and secretions are the world of the hormonal space. We experience this space all the time. It's both our emotional state and the whole background tone of the body and mind. Learning to attune to this space means opening up to your biochemical nature. The biggest thing going off in our bodies is its biochemistry; in many ways, it's all there is. The body structure is a physical manifestation of the chemical processes taking place in the remarkable saltwater medium of the body.

THE SEA INSIDE THE BODY

The sea inside us makes for a perfect chemical solution. Water acts as the ultimate molecular matrix in which all other substances interact. This is where the mix of electrolytes, hormones, immune cell secretions and neuropeptides all interact. It's the hormonal soup of the body that contains NEI substances, that is, secretions of the nervous system (N), the endocrine system (E) and the immune system (I), so that all of them interact with the cells of the body. Structurally, that brings the brain, glands and immune cells into deep communion. It's the body's messengers and communication pathways that constantly bring about changes in cell activity and their production (Figure 14.1). It's complex, but just look at the arrows and not so much at the diagram labelling to see the intercommunication that is going on in our bodies. No wonder it's taking so long to fully understand human biology.

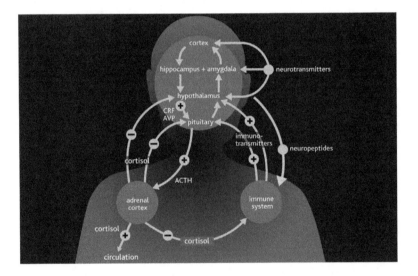

Figure 14.1 NEI orchestra

Everything the body does is driven by these substances. Some of them act on every cell of the body, while some act quite specifically on only certain groups of cells.

Without getting lost in the endless details of this aspect of the body, there are a few important things to appreciate in terms of felt sense awareness:

- The fluid system is an NEI fluid. It's not just water or salt water; it's a mix of all these substances, that is, a mix of molecules.

- The fluid body has qualities of all of these molecules which you can discern.

- Glands produce hormonal spaces.

- Immune cells have a signature.

- The brain produces neuropeptides and neurotransmitters which we feel all the time. We are awash in them.

If we start to experience our fluid body as a NEI-active fluid, we can start to discern the incredible dynamic molecular energy of it. There are some wonderfully illuminating meditations below that offer insight into this vibrancy. The molecularity of this fluid space, the interstitial space, is a mad mix of all kinds of sizes, shapes and vibrational qualities of molecules. They are all suspended in a saltwater matrix that supports an electrostatic relational field perfect for reactivity.

We can likewise follow the hormonal array of some of the body's endocrine glands through this series of meditations, which will help us connect with each gland and its hormonal space. These are the primary energies of the body, and you can start to appreciate the huge power of hormones and how distinct each one is. All the hormones make us feel certain emotional and perceptual states. For example, oxytocin, serotonin and melatonin are all powerful drugs produced by the body to make us happy and blissful.

The important thing to understand about the endocrine system is that it's not just about glands. The gland is the secretory mechanism, but the expression of the gland is the hormone that is active in the interstitial fluid space. This space is where the cells are and therefore where the cell receptors are. The interaction of all hormones is with cell receptors, which are generally long-chain peptides extending from the cell membrane like tentacles. There are thousands of these receptors on each cell, making the surface of the cell hairy and not smooth as they are often imagined to be.

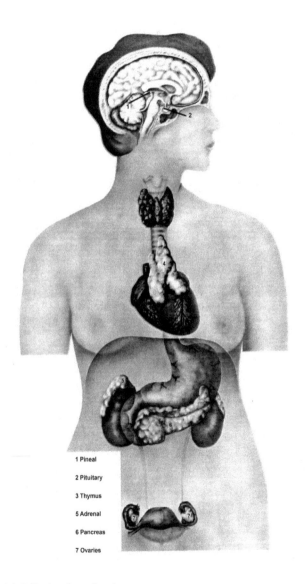

1 Pineal

2 Pituitary

3 Thymus

5 Adrenal

6 Pancreas

7 Ovaries

Figure 14.2 Endocrine glands

The way that receptors and hormones come together and bond has to do with their shape and their vibration. Once there is a bonding, there is a change in the receptor that generates a signal cascade through the membrane and then through the whole cell to the nucleus and the DNA. So the hormone could be asking the cell to increase production of mucus, and the signal cascade will lead to accessing of genes for the sequence of mucus, which the cell then manufactures from this blueprint. With stress and trauma these receptors can become literally bent out of shape such that hormones can no longer bond with them, so the cell starts to drop out of contact with the NEI system.

The meditations below have to do with connecting the glands, circulatory system and interstitial fluids. This constitutes the hormonal space.

PITUITARY GLAND

The pituitary is one of the smallest glands in the body. It produces a huge array of hormones that control many functions directly or through other glands. The pituitary influences growth, blood pressure, breast milk production, sexual function, thyroid function, some aspects of birth and pregnancy, metabolism, water regulation, temperature control and pain relief.

The gland is located in a fascinating place. It hangs off the underside of the brain like a small grape or olive and nestles in a hollow in the sphenoid bone right at the centre of the cranial base. The sphenoid has grown around it to protect it. The internal carotid artery enters the cranium just by the side of the pituitary and receives the first fresh blood before it flows to the brain.

Meditation: finding your pituitary

Feel the volume and fluidity to the eyes and follow the path of light as it moves through the cornea and lens to the retina. Feel the unique photosensitive cells at the back of the eye and how the optic nerve tingles along its length. Follow it back to the optic chiasm, which is where the optic fibres cross. The optic chiasm sits right in front of the pituitary. The optic nerves move around the pituitary. This is a useful way to find the pituitary with accuracy. The other way is to follow the arterial flow up through your neck into your cranial base. The carotid weaves through two holes in the cranial base and forms an arterial circle (known as the circle of Willis) around the pituitary and creates a capillary bed into the pituitary. Feel the energy and dynamism of your pituitary. This is your most active gland. Follow its secretions into the venous return, through the jugular veins back to the heart and from there through the whole system to the capillary beds and the space between cells. This is the hormonal space of the pituitary hormones.

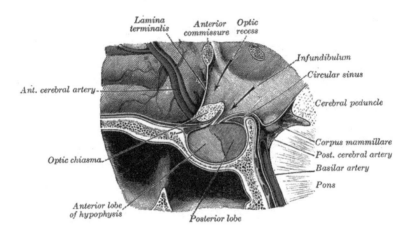

Figure 14.3 Pituitary gland

PINEAL GLAND

The pineal gland is a small endocrine gland in the brain at the back of the third ventricle. It produces the serotonin derivative melatonin, a hormone that affects the modulation of wake/sleep patterns and seasonal functions.

The pineal gland lies at the back of the third ventricle and in the upper cistern of the cerebellum, so it's surrounded by cerebrospinal fluid. This is very different from the pituitary, which sits in the sphenoid with a diaphragm over the top of it.

Melatonin is a hormone that brings the body into alignment with nature through the light-and-dark cycle, and that makes it concerned with the environment in which we live. It adjusts the body in relation to the world outside. Most other hormones respond to internal cell needs, so that difference sets melatonin and the pineal gland apart.

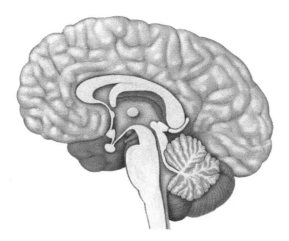

Figure 14.4 Pineal gland

Meditation: opening up your pineal gland

The core of your brain comprises a fluid space called the third ventricle. Don't focus on it, but allow it to come into your awareness. It's best if you are in whole-body awareness. The pineal gland projects out from the back of this fluid space. Now follow your optic nerves past the pituitary to the brain stem where the optic nerves synapse at the lateral geniculate nuclei, which are on either side of the pineal gland. This is how the pineal gland derives its information about light and dark. The pituitary gland is embedded in bones and membrane. The pineal gland is surrounded on both sides by cerebrospinal fluid and has, therefore, a very different environment. The interventricular circulatory system brings blood to and from the pineal. Follow the flow of melatonin as it is secreted throughout the body. It starts to secrete when the Sun goes down (Figure 14.5).

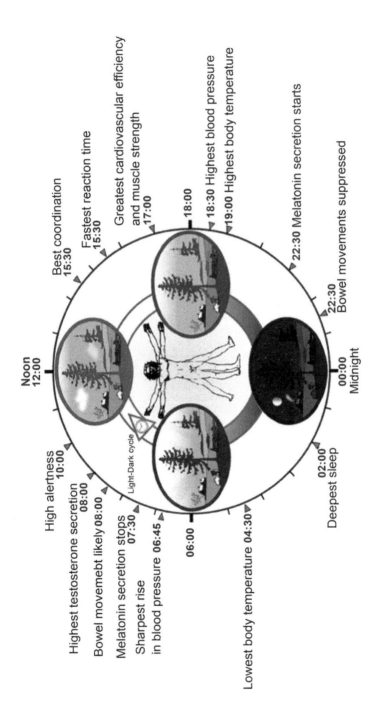

Figure 14.5 Circadian rhythms

THYROID GLAND

The thyroid gland controls how quickly the body uses energy, makes proteins and controls how sensitive the body is to other hormones. The thyroid produces triiodothryroxine (T3) and thyroxine (T4). These hormones regulate the rate of metabolism and affect the growth and rate of function of many other systems in the body. The thyroid essentially controls the speed of the cells, so when it gets out of control, it creates havoc.

The thyroid also produces calcitonin, which plays a role in calcium homeostasis along with parathyroid hormone secreted by four little buttons on the back of the thyroid called the parathyroid glands. These two hormones are responsible for the take up and laying down of calcium in the bones.

Thyroid hormones play a particularly crucial role in brain maturation during foetal development.

The pituitary affects the thyroid by producing a hormone called thyroid-stimulating hormone (TSH), which prompts the thyroid to release more T4 and T3. If there is too much thyroxine circulating in the blood, the pituitary reduces the amount of TSH produced, which causes thyroid activity to slow. If there is too little thyroxine, the pituitary increases the amount of TSH. In this way, T4 and T3 levels in the blood are kept relatively constant. The pituitary gland, in turn, is overseen by a part of the brain called the hypothalamus. This is a dynamic process that depends on the NEI working well together.

It is common for people to have overactive or underactive thyroid glands. The thyroid controls heat and metabolism. If it is overactive, people can be too thin, nervous, quick, agitated and sweaty. If it is underactive, people tend to be slow in action and thought, cold and gain weight.

Meditation: thyroid

The thyroid is in an unlikely place: right at the centre of our throat. The body is indeed mysterious, but clearly part of the reason is that it's at the centre of two powerful blood flows. Glands love being near rich blood supplies. In fact, the thyroid hangs off the carotid and jugular veins. Coming into felt sense awareness of it is easy. Simply bring your awareness down from your mouth and jaw and glide down the front of the throat, and it's located at the bottom of the throat just above the sternal notch (the depression just above the sternum). The throat is a mix of muscle, cartilage and bone, and then suddenly there's quite a different feeling of glandular cells. They are completely enmeshed in a rich capillary network.

Sit with the feeling of your thyroid. How active does it feel? The main secretion is thyroxine, so the tone of the gland will be the felt sense of thyroxine. Follow it through the circulatory system to all the cells. This is the hormonal space for the thyroid. Stay with it.

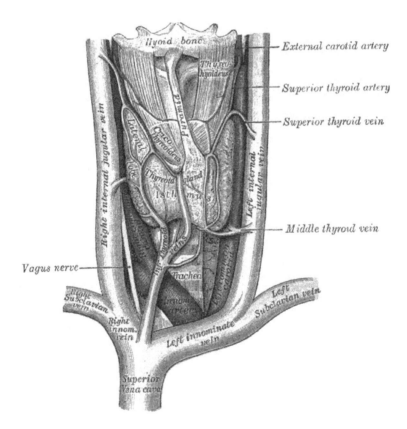

Figure 14.6 Thyroid

PANCREAS

The pancreas is remarkable in that it is both a digestive gland and an endocrine gland. It is the biggest gland in the body and secretes pancreatic juice into the duodenum, which is a mix of enzymes that break down carbohydrates, proteins and lipids. The pancreas also produces an array of hormones that maintain blood glucose levels, namely, insulin (decreases glucose in blood), glucagon (increases glucose in blood) and somatostatin (regulates both).

The pancreas is situated deep in the body against the back wall of the upper abdominal cavity, behind the peritoneum, and it lies transverse from the duodenum (head) to the spleen (tail). It is a highly active, vital organ that contributes to two of the most powerful needs of the body: to break down food and to maintain glucose levels in the blood. Both functions are about delivering raw material to the cell for metabolic processes.

The pancreas is, interestingly, one of those structures in the body to which most people don't have a felt sense relationship. We can feel our heart and lungs, gut and liver, bladder and kidneys, but the pancreas is hidden deep within the core of the body and its activity is not distinguishable from what is taking place around it. Perhaps it is *meant* to be hidden. It takes a while to open up a felt sense perspective of the pancreas. The best time is just after eating food, when the pancreas is particularly active in both its main functions.

Sadly, this is one of the glands that is seriously affected by modern life. Habits of overeating, and taking in too much sugar in particular, put the pancreas under pressure, and therefore there is a clearly charted increase in pancreatic conditions, none of which are mild.

Meditation: pancreas

This is one of those meditations when it's best to meditate *after* you've eaten. The pancreas erupts into activity as both and endocrine and exocrine gland when you eat, so you can't miss it. It's underneath and deep to the right of the stomach in the middle of your torso (nearer the back wall of the torso). You can feel the pancreas as a long, cylindrical object at the centre of the torso. After you eat, the major hormonal secretion is insulin, so when you open up to the interstitial space, you are in touch with the feeling of insulin. Each hormone has a characteristic tone in the body. Sitting with the pancreas can be highly regulating for a gland that works so hard. Feel the power of the pancreas.

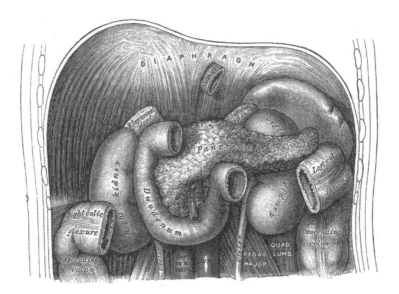

Figure 14.7 Pancreas

ADRENAL GLANDS

The adrenal gland is our fight-or-flight gland that produces adrenaline and cortisol. Cortisol is a chemical released when we are under stress at high levels. Long-term secretion can be dangerous because it interrupts transmission of messages from neuron to neuron and creates a whole series of undesirable systemic effects. Stress caused by high levels of cortisol is becoming increasingly common in our society.

Below is a summary of the effects of cortisol on the body:

- Decreases immune activity:
  - Inflammation is suppressed.
  - The ability to fight infections is downgraded.
  - It has other complex effects on immune activity.
- Mobilizes energy:
  - It shuts down sugar storage and uptake of sugar everywhere, except in exercising muscles.
  - It has the opposite action to insulin.
- Increases tone of the cardiovascular system:
  - It shuts down peripheral blood.
  - It increases blood to exercising muscles, heart and brain.
- Decreases digestion:
  - Peristalsis and secretions are reduced.
  - Secretion of growth hormone is inhibited.
  - Reproductive hormones are inhibited.
- Sharpens cognition:
  - The senses are heightened.

Generally, these are alarming effects that can lead to collapse of energy levels and vital functions; therefore, you need to be able to recognize these symptoms and take steps to turn off the secretion.

Meditation: adrenal medulla and cortex

The adrenal glands have an inner and outer layer. The outer layer or cortex is where cortisol is produced, and the inner layer or medulla is where adrenaline and noradrenaline are produced. The adrenal glands are above the kidneys and under the diaphragm. The easiest way to locate them is to bring your awareness to the back of your lower ribcage. The most distinctive feeling in the area comes from direct enervation of the medulla. This is a unique nervous connection from sympathetic nerve fibres coming through the solar plexus and the sympathetic chain. It's a special part of your nervous system that allows your hypothalamus to directly turn on your adrenal medulla to produce adrenaline. The glandular cells literally get electrified into action and there's an instant response. Arousal of these cells over time generates a distinctive feel that means the medulla is activated. Notice how your medulla feels. Notice the difference between left and right. Simply being with the felt sense awareness of this part of the adrenal glands will help regulate the nervous excitation and turn off the secretion of adrenaline.

Now shift your awareness to the outer layer of the adrenals. There's a distinct change in sensations. This part of the gland is involved in cortisol production. The pituitary secretes a hormone that controls the secretion of cortisol, so the outer layer of the cortex doesn't feel electrical. If these glandular cells are activated, you are experiencing cortisol. As with the medulla, being present with the adrenal cortex, circulatory system and interstitial fluid space will help regulate the action of the gland.

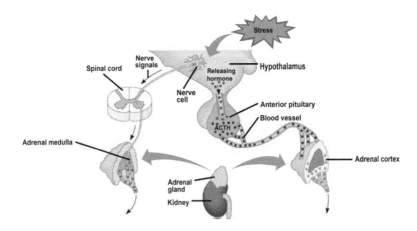

Figure 14.8 Adrenal stress

NEUROTRANSMITTERS

Neurotransmitters are powerful chemicals that regulate numerous physical and emotional processes such as mental performance, emotional states and pain response. Virtually all functions in life are controlled by neurotransmitters. They are the brain's chemical messengers. Interactions between neurotransmitters, hormones and the brain's chemicals have a profound influence on overall health and well-being.

When our concentration and focus are good, we feel more directed, motivated and vibrant. Unfortunately, if neurotransmitter levels are inadequate, these energizing and motivating signals are absent and we feel more stressed, sluggish and out of control.

Neurotransmitters do the following tasks:

- control the appetite centre of the brain

- stimulate corticotropin-releasing factor, adrenocorticotropic hormone and cortisol

- regulate male and female sex hormones

- regulate sleep

- modulate mood and thought processes

- control the ability to focus, concentrate and remember things.

Neurotransmitters affect the limbic system, which controls the body's autonomic levels, and the hypothalamus, which controls the pituitary and therefore the whole endocrine cascade. In other words, the neurons of the brain secrete substances that regulate the functions of the glands in the rest of the body. The main pathway through which this regulation occurs passes through the pituitary gland, whose hormones influence practically all of the other glands in the body.

Intelligence is a distributed phenomenon mediated by a vast communicating network of chemicals and cells. Intelligence is not solely a top-down affair from the central nervous system. The NEI tells us how we think and feel, which influences what happens in our body, and what happens in our body determines how we think and feel. The brain, a 'bag of hormones', and the chemical interactions in the central nervous system are of far greater significance than the electrical activity.

Neurotransmitters are the hormones of the brain. Electrical charges from the cell body free chemicals and propel them across the synapse. Special receptors at the end of dendrites form to accept certain neurotransmitters like a lock and key. Just as chicken soup makes your body feel better, chemicals produced in your brain make *it* feel better. These chemicals (over 60 different kinds) affect memory, learning and relationships. The thoughts we have, the food we eat and the drugs we take all have an effect on the chemicals in our brains. Different neurotransmitters affect brain activity in different ways.

Important neurotransmitters

SEROTONIN

Serotonin aids in the smooth transmission of messages in the brain and body. It plays an important role in the regulation of mood, appetite, memory and learning. It is commonly associated with feelings of well-being and happiness. A lack of serotonin may result in low self-esteem, depression and/or aggression.

DOPAMINE

Dopamine helps information flow to higher levels in the brain. It plays a key role in regulating pain and pleasure as well as a major role in reward-motivated behaviour.

MELATONIN

Melatonin relates to wake and sleep cycles.

EPINEPHRINE

Epinephrine gets the body moving in situations that require instant action, such as those involving fear or danger.

ACETYLCHOLINE

Acetylcholine enhances memory. (It is the chemical responsible for many dreams.)

ENDORPHINS

Endorphins are the body's natural pain killer. They are opium-derived peptides that function as neurotransmitters. They are produced by the pituitary and hypothalamus during exercise, excitement, pain, spicy-food consumption as well as love and sexual activity. They resemble opiates in their ability to produce analgesia and a feeling of well-being.

Meditation: serotonin

Bring your awareness to your small intestine. Ninety per cent of serotonin in the body is secreted by cells in the gut lining that are responsible for smooth peristaltic motion. Listen to your peristalsis. The gut generates a ripple-like movement along its length. Optimal peristalsis is a sign of healthy serotonin production. Use Figure 14.9 to connect with your felt sense awareness of serotonin. Now shift your awareness to your brain, and once again, open up to the feeling of serotonin. If you keep repeating this meditation the body secretes the hormone at more balanced levels, resulting in greater feelings of happiness and mood stability.

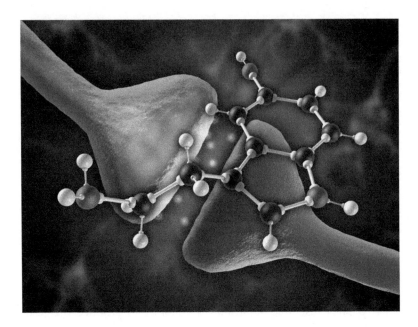

Figure 14.9 Serotonin

IMMUNE SYSTEM

Where is the immune system? It's not as simple to locate as individual structures. Of course there are immune system organs, such as the lymphatics, spleen and tonsils, but really the immune system comprises the collection of all WBCs, which are located in many different places in the body and are mostly free, not fixed (in the blood, lymphatic system, spleen, under the skin and freely moving in connective tissues). If we were to put these WBCs together in one mass and call them an immune organ, it would be as big as a kidney! The immune cells secrete a whole array of substances that affect neurons and glandular cells as well as many other body cells. Here are some of their names: interleukins, cytokines, chemokines, interferons and lymphokines.

The neuroendocrine regulation of the inflammatory response is of major significance from the point of view of immune homeostasis. Malfunction of this circuit leads to disease and often is life-threatening. Chronic stress changes gene activity in immune cells before they reach the bloodstream. With these changes, the cells are primed to fight an infection or trauma that doesn't actually exist, leading to an overabundance of chronic inflammation that is linked to many health problems.

Prolonged experience of psychological stress shifts the balance from cell-mediated (T cell) to overactive humoral-mediated activity (B cell). Stress, therefore, weakens our ability to combat viruses and cancer, for example, and we are more likely to overreact to threats. So we mount unnecessary or prolonged mucosal defences (which renders us more susceptible to allergies, asthma, upper respiratory tract infections, gastrointestinal inflammatory conditions and cystitis, for example).

On the plus side, immune cells are some of our most powerful cells, and any kind of felt sense connection to them is a remarkable feeling. One of the most powerful monocytes is the macrophage. These cells are experts at breaking down unwanted cells such as bacteria or worn-out RBCs. Many of them are freely moving around the body, but there are also large communities of them in our lymph nodes and spleen.

Meditation: macrophage

Look at Figure 14.10. The macrophage is one of your most powerful immune cells. There are large populations in the spleen and lymph glands as well as unfixed macrophages moving around the body. The cells engulf microbes and secrete substances that break down the cell membrane. Macrophages are also involved in wound healing. Use the image to open up to the felt sense of the macrophage population in your body. There is a particular feeling generated from this meditation – the macrophage produces a unique signature in the body's felt sense, which you can learn to feel. Repeating the meditation is a way to strengthen your immune system.

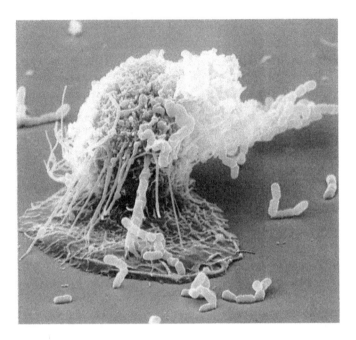

Figure 14.10 Macrophage

CHAPTER 15

Brain Balancing

The brain is in a state of balanced chaos. The nature of neurons is to be independent as well as social, but it's a lot to expect 100 billion of them to cooperate and run smoothly. The brain is starting to be understood more and more deeply, and it's clearly not as hierarchical and ordered as biologists once thought. It is also becoming clear that the brain is highly elastic. Even in adults the brain can be reshaped by events. Chronic pain studies have revealed how the brain can remap itself. Behaving in different ways can bring about structural changes in the brain. This all indicates that the brain can be influenced and is adaptive.

THE NATURE OF THE BRAIN

The brain is reflective of our cultural and social conditioning. The way we turn out is not just down to genetics. Human culture has a huge effect on brain development. Neuroscience and attachment theory have tracked the effects of the early caregiving environment on the physiological development of the brain. Traumatic childhoods generate chaotic, imbalanced brains, whereas stable, loving childhoods generate balanced brains. Brain imbalance leads to neurotic behaviour, chronic inflammation and hypersensitivity. It can also lead to psychotic pathologies.

Babies and children have to learn to generate balance in their nervous systems, and consequentially their emotional and behavioural expressions take a whole childhood to mature into a synthesized expression. There's a period of balance in our lives when we mature and lead an adult life but then the brain starts to lose its coherency and returns to chaos. Out of chaos has come order, and from that order we go back to chaos.

There are a lot of reasons why the brain may be struggling to regulate itself and, therefore, the rest of our body. (Modern society gives it a lot to think about!) The level of stress experienced by the average person in the Western world is hundreds of times that of our recent forefathers. There's pressure on our brains. Brains are behaving as if they are in a state of survival, which is not healthy. Our brains need our help.

An important fact to comprehend is that the brain is a unit – it's one brain. Although science divides the brain into parts to study it and to observe it as a functional composite, the more you can acknowledge the oneness of your brain, the better. Modern brain-scanning techniques impressively demonstrate just how complex the brain actually is. For example, they reveal how certain areas of the brain light up as we think or act. It's just not as simple as that lit-up section being all about anger, or movement of your arm, or thinking about food. The brain is a network just like the environment is a network. Interconnectedness is how the brain functions. Whole rafts of fibres and nuclei switch on and off as we speak, think and move. It's like there are a million light bulbs in there!

The brain involves a matrix of relationships. It contains almost an infinite number of synapses, although it is grooved. We pattern it with our experiences and our repetitive behaviour; however, as we know, its nature is to be mutable. You can help yourself think and behave differently to generate brain balance. Coming into your sensory system and generating new sensations through felt sense meditation is a great way to develop and reform neural pathways. It's exciting to know that we can change our thinking and behaviour.

Meditation: one brain

The brain is whole in its functionality, so coming into felt sense awareness of its wholeness will help the neural flow become smoother, and the different parts of it will move together in a synthesized way (Figure 15.1).

Start at your head. Let your awareness sink through the outer layer of bone and membrane to find the mass of the brain. Try not to be focused as you do this. It's better to be spacious with your awareness and allow the brain to find you. Open up a listening space for the qualities and textures of the brain as a tissue landscape to reveal itself. The softer and more peripheral your attention, the more depth and subtlety comes to you about the body.

Now open up to the length of the spinal cord. This is the tail of the brain and part of its wholeness. Being with both brain and spinal cord generates a different feeling experience. It brings length but also brings connection into the depth of the body through the peripheral nervous system. Encourage all the roots and branches of the nerve fibres of the peripheral nervous system to enter into the spinal cord relationship. The brain has its tendrils in all parts of the body.

As you stay with the one-brain feeling, relax into your fluid body. This allows the nervous system to soften and regulate around its inner and outer fluid mechanisms. The feeling is of deep relaxation across the whole nervous system.

Having acknowledged the oneness of the brain, we can now see that the brain is composed of some powerful parts that can create huge imbalances throughout the body. The brain is immensely complex, but let's cut through all of that and simply say that it's composed of five major parts: two cerebral hemispheres, one cerebellum, one brain stem which includes the spinal cord and one limbic system at the very core of the brain. Each chunk has its own physiology and functionality that determines many aspects of the nervous system and therefore whole-body balance.

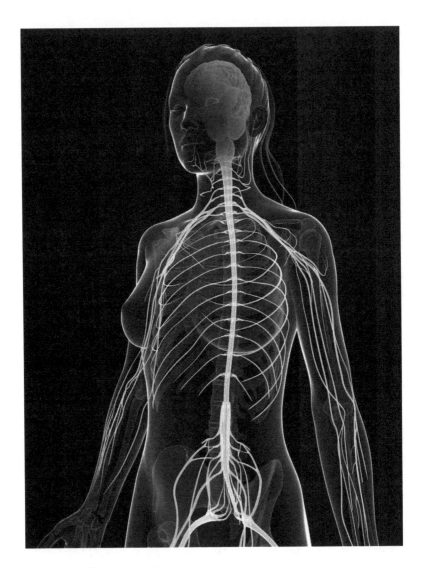

Figure 15.1 Nervous system

Meditation: cerebral hemisphere

The hemispheres are actually one of the biggest structures in your body. They are the most active structures in the cranium and are therefore easy to recognize. There's a massive hum of electrical activity going on under your crown. We think from the hemispheres, we move our body from here and we interpret the outside world from here. In addition, all things around language are processed here, of course, so it's a busy place (Figure 15.2).

Invite a sense of the hemispheres into your awareness. Here you'll find a sense of a mass along with a feeling of activity. There's also a fluid membranous tone which has to do with the surrounding fluid and membranes that help support the hemispheres. Notice how the left and right hemispheres feel different from each other. What is the nervous tone of your hemispheres? Do they feel hyped up or at ease in their activity? Stay with them in relationship to the whole brain/spinal cord phenomenon. Recognizing the inter-relatedness of the central nervous system is deeply healing.

Now open up to the left and right sides of your body. What does this bring about in the hemispheres? You are opening up to the many fibre pathways that move through the brain and into the spinal cord, into your periphery and back. That is a powerful awareness state.

Now open up the corpus callosum, which is the bridge between the two hemispheres. It's a communication pathway that allows both hemispheres to interact and inform each other. This can be quite intriguing. The bridge between the hemispheres is a very active place, and maintaining your awareness of these structures can help regulate neural pathways.

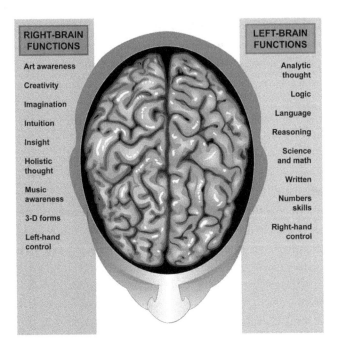

Figure 15.2 The cerebral hemispheres

THE EYES

Meditation: eye–brain state

Hold the back of your head with the palm of a hand. Underneath the bones in the cerebrum are the optic centres in your brain. These centres receive a flow of electrical impulses from your eyes that they interpret in order to give you the sense of sight. Now close both your eyes. Notice the change in sensations in your hand. Now open both eyes. Can you feel the difference? Electrical impulses are flowing towards your hand from the action of light on the retina of the eyes. Now close both eyes and try opening just one eye. Part of the impulses from each eye cross over to the other side of the brain, so you should feel part of the occipital lobe light up on either side. (It should be more on one side.) Try the other eye now. What you are feeling is the combined effect of tens of thousands of neurons.

The eyes are fascinating. The whole optic array of the eyes traverses the brain from front to back: optic nerves, optic chiasm, lateral geniculate nuceli at the top of the brain stem and the optic centres in the occipital lobe of the cerebrum. This is a unique horizontal pathway right across the brain. The brain and the eyes have a profound effect on each other. The eyes have grown out of the brain and could be considered to be the part of the brain that is showing itself to the world. If the brain becomes aroused and irritated, the eyes can be deeply affected. Lots of visual issues may well have to do with the general state of the brain rather than the sense organ itself. The eye is a very useful way to help the brain as a whole decelerate and become calm. Letting tension dissolve in and around your eyes will regulate the flow into the optic nerves and soften all the parts of the brain with which the optics are connected. The optic nerves cross over in front of the pituitary, connect with the brain stem and flow into the cerebral cortex (Figure 15.3).

Meditation: the eyes

Try winding the eyes down by bringing your felt sense awareness to the whole body, and within the wholeness, feel the state of your eyes. How relaxed are they? Spend several minutes relaxing your eyes and feel the effects throughout your body and nervous system. Keep your eyes open and let go of focusing. Drop into your peripheral vision.

Now let the muscles of your eyes relax. Small oblique and rectus muscles surround the eyes and are attached to the orbit and sclera of the eye. As you let the muscles relax, the eyes should start to feel relaxed as well. Now be interested in the fluid of the eyes. This is the largest part of the eyes. As you become more aware of the inner fluid chambers, the eyes start to feel more fluid-like. Let this happen and be aware that your vision may become slightly blurry.

Now close your eyes and follow the pathways of the optic nerves with your felt sense. Stay with a connection to your whole body. Neurons are cells just like muscle cells, and they are surrounded by connective tissues. Let these cells wind down in the nerve fibres all the way back to the synapses at the brain stem, and then follow again to the cerebral cortex in the occipital lobe. Let the visual nuclei wind down.

Now be interested in the motor nerves originating from the brain stem. Do the same procedure with them. Literally follow them with your awareness, letting them wind down as they move forward through the sphenoid to the eye muscles. Become aware of the rest of your body. What has changed? How's your breathing and heart rate? How's your nervous system tone?

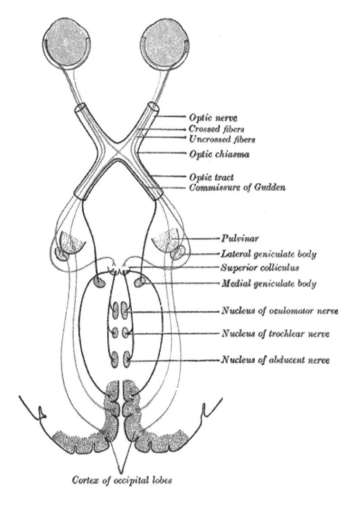

Figure 15.3 Optics

THE BRAIN STEM AND ACTIVATION

The brain stem contains nuclei that control the autonomic nervous system. There's a 'magic inch' in the middle of the stem. In this region there are nuclei that control heart rate, brain arousal, breathing, digestion and many of the special senses.

There is a direct neural signal to the adrenal glands from the brain stem. Sympathetic nerves connect directly into the adrenal medulla. This causes adrenaline and noradrenaline to be released into the bloodstream within fractions of a second in response to a stressor. This surge of adrenaline gears the body up for activity, that is, we go into fight-or-flight mode.

Parasympathetic activity is also mediated through the brain stem. In overwhelming stress, brain stem nuclei, in response to limbic system signals, trigger the release of endorphins. The endorphins flood the central nervous system, inhibiting incoming signals. This is the freeze or dissociation response.

The brain stem can be perceived as being like the stalk of a cauliflower, below and deep to the cerebral hemispheres. It can be perceived as a highly active area in the brain connecting the fluid ventricles and the huge cerebral hemispheres into the information superhighway of the spinal cord.

Simply by orienting to the brain stem, appreciating its connections to the whole body and supporting the natural urge to regulation, we can allow profound change in our physiology.

The brain stem is a very powerful portal into working with facilitation of the whole central nervous system. Facilitation describes the process where parts of the nervous system become overly sensitive and overly active. This is often due to aberrant incoming sensory information (for example, from traumatic events, joints being out of position, organ inflammation or tight connective tissues).

Meditation: portals of the sympathetic nervous system

The following steps are about exploring the quality and feel of the sympathetic nervous system from different portals. They are used in a diagnostic sense, and they are useful to confirm that the system is busy or that it has changed. With experience, a characteristic sympathetic buzz will become very familiar. This is the nervous tone. When there is regulation and neurons relax, the buzz changes pitch and becomes lower. A shrill sound equals a high nervous tone, which indicates that the neurons are getting overly excited.

Orient to the brain stem. The area under the back of your head, near the top of the neck, is the lower brain of the brain stem and cerebellum. Open up to deep structures, tissue quality and tone in this area. Underneath the bony layer it feels fluid and electrical. There is a lot of cerebrospinal fluid in this area, bathing the busy brain stem and cerebellum. You know when you have contacted the brain stem, as there is suddenly a feeling of continuity with the spinal cord. Connect with the area for a couple of minutes before moving to the next portal.

Now shift your awareness to the ganglion of impar at the other end of the sympathetic chains, directly in front of the coccyx. There will be a unique feeling here that will include the bony coccyx and the pelvic floor, of which it is a part. The intention is to be interested in the nervous energy. Again, stay with it for a couple of minutes and move up to the series of plexi that lie in the visceral cavities in front of the vertebral column. Start with locating the hypogastric plexus. This is like a control box for the lower pelvic viscera. Spend 2 minutes being in felt sense awareness of it, then move your awareness up to the enteric plexus in the gut. Notice the sensations coming from here and notice, too, what happens when you simply offer a neutral listening.

Now move your awareness up to the solar plexus and then to the cardiac plexus in the chest. Finally, find the tops of the sympathetic chains at the top of your neck. The ganglia sit just lateral to the vertebral bodies.

This whole process should take around 15 minutes. Be curious about the different portals. They all have characteristic expressions of nervous energy. This meditation will help balance the whole sympathetic flow and will feel like your system is winding down. With repetition you will train this part of the nervous system to regulate back to balanced tone, and your experience will move away from anxiety and feeling overwhelmed into peace and quiet.

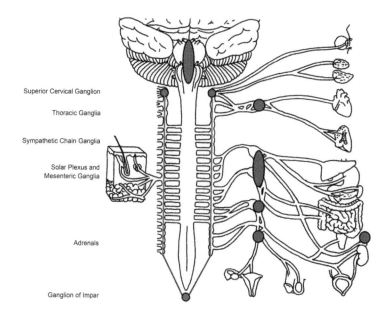

Figure 15.4 ANS portals

CHAPTER 16

Life Continuum

We are part of a system. We are animals living in an ecosystem on a planet. We are remarkable in what we have accomplished, but we are still governed by forces such as gravity, age and physical drives. In fact, our biggest drives are all internal and physical. We need to be in relationships, be touched, have sex as well as drink, eat and do other things in order to survive. All animals have these drives. We are a product of nature, so let's just accept that. We want to be special, but we are, in fact, just a part of the tapestry of life. So let's revel in our animal nature. Let's get to know ourselves as creatures of flesh that are part of a dynamic ecosystem.

Nothing is separate from the ecosystem. Opening up to our environment means opening up to our body's connection to the life around us. We are not separate. We are in the continuum of life that stretches out across the planet and out to the stars. How our bodies are connected to the universe is an amazing thing. If we can become intimate with this connection, we can start to drop into our place in nature and stop imagining that we are separate from it – or even superior to it.

Every day we talk about the weather, we eat food grown in the earth, drink water from the planet and breathe the air. Natural disasters make headlines every day. The planet's activities dominate our lives. When we open up to the huge flow of connection that we have with our surroundings, we start to appreciate how dynamic our body can be in the field of nature. When the mind embraces this, something very deep happens: we merge with nature. The struggle to be separate and autonomous is killing us. We are holding back from the nurturing of life in and around us.

Our bodies were formed in utero, and then we were born and looked after. It was effortless: we surrendered to life and it formed us and adapted us. Let's embrace that flow of life again, because it hasn't gone away; it's still running our bodies. We never need to think about digesting and breathing and circulating. It's all being done by the rhythm and deep intelligence of life within us.

CONNECTING WITH NATURE
Meditation: horizon

Our relationship to the ocean is so deep that we only have to think about it to create an effect. Even if you are in the middle of a busy city, the effects are palpable.

Sitting comfortably, bring to mind a beach or coast that you find uplifting. Let the image reveal details and follow the shift in body mood and tone. Now imagine that you are there and you are looking out to sea, watching the movements of the ocean as the waves rise and fall. Follow the waves in to shore. Imagine that you are wading into the sea and that the sea is warm to the skin. Now you are floating on the sea. Finally, come out of the sea and sit in a comfortable chair with a sun umbrella behind you and look out towards the horizon. Observe how the edge of the sea blends with the beginning of the sky. Scan across the whole horizon and back and few times. Once again, notice the effect on your body.

Let go of the visualization and sit with the sense of your fluid body and notice how energized you feel.

Meditation: forest

As you proceed through this meditation, you will be tracking your body and mind responses with precision.

Sitting comfortably, imagine that you are walking through a forest. Come into an open glade at the centre of the forest and sit in the shade at the edge. Feel the forest floor under you as you find a comfortable sitting position. Be part of the forest. Take in the smells and the movement and the quality of the air. You are breathing the forest in. Your body is sensing the forest, so it's about coming into the subtleties of your senses.

Open up to the immediate space around you. That includes the air and the ground and the trees. As you acknowledge this environment, you will experience a shift in your body tone and texture. Stay with it for a few minutes and then open up to a much more expanded perceptual field. Be inclusive in this movement to a wider field. Rather than pushing your mind out, have an attitude of inviting the forest into your field of awareness so that the forest comes to *you* rather than you expanding out to *it*.

Your body, the forest and the air are all in a continuum of life. Again, stay with that for a few minutes and notice the physical changes that the perceptual shift precipitates. Finally, open up to the whole ecosystem. Feel yourself as a part of the environment. Our skin makes us feel separate, so at the same time imagine your skin as something that is permeable. Let the barrier of your skin soften so that the outline of your body starts to merge with the environment. Notice any fear that arises. Letting your skin dissolve opens up an experience of oneness with nature. Quite a different feeling emerges in your body as this takes place. Sit and be neutral to the experience of it.